INTRODUCTION

DEMOCRACY AND LEADERSHIP: A WAY OF LIFE

A lot of people think that **democracy** is about politics and governance while **leadership** is about politics and business. And they are right. However, there is more to democracy and leadership than politics, governance and business. Democracy and leadership are also about life in general.

During our work with democracy and leadership over some time, it has gradually dawned on us that the values and attitudes that underpin real democracy and good leadership also are very much present in decent everyday human life. Summed up in one concept the common ground is **human dignity**. The aim of this book is therefore to clarify how human dignity may be a guiding star in our lives. Hopefully that clarification will inspire the reader to lead an active, participative life both privately and publicly and see democracy and leadership as efficient vehicles to realize this good life on individual as well as community level.

A textbook

This book is designed as a textbook to be used for introductory courses about democracy and leadership. Therefore there are some study questions at the end of each chapter. We believe that time spent working on these questions will enhance the reader's benefit considerably.

The structure and main content of the book

The book is organized in three parts. **Part One** focuses on democracy and is written by Odd Ragnar Hunnes. **Part Two** is about leadership, written by Michael Flowers. Co-written by the authors, **Part Three** combines democracy and leadership.

The chapters in the book constitute a whole and therefore there are cross-references between them. At the same time we have intended that each chapter also may be read separately. Therefore some pieces of information or points may appear in more than one chapter.

PART ONE: DEMOCRACY

Chapter One: So what is Democracy?
In this chapter a variety of aspects of democracy are presented, and this includes dimensions and foundations of democracy as well as dilemmas. Being strong believers in the advantages of democracy, we are also aware of a number of challenges that need to be met. One of the most important is to secure that democratic values, attitudes, ways and means are strengthened in each society and each generation. Therefore, school is given some special attention.

Chapter Two: Human Dignity – The Core Value of Democracy
This chapter points to what we believe is the core value, the foundation of democracy: human dignity. A former prime minister of Norway recently declared that democracy is a natural consequence of human dignity. The point is that human dignity is a matter of good values, attitudes and acts that benefit the individual as well as society. Democracy offers a 'system' for how to live socially in accordance with such values. And as this is done, human dignity in the actual society is strengthened.

Chapter Three: Is Democracy (only) a Western Concept?
Here the notion that democracy in essence is a Western concept is addressed. It is sometimes claimed that promotion of democracy, intentionally or unintentionally, is in effect a promotion of Western ideas, ideals and influence into other parts of the world. Since the authors have close links with Africa, this chapter highlights some examples of African culture which indicate that democracy is far from foreign to the continent. The chapter concludes that since democracy is very much intertwined with society's culture, as a consequence we should expect different societies to realize democracy somewhat

differently. The quintessence is that it is founded on and promotes human dignity, and that should be a universal ideal.

PART TWO: LEADERSHIP

Chapter Four: Understanding Leadership
Recognising that there is an element of leadership characteristics in every individual, this chapter is intended to stimulate the reader's understanding of the subject-matter. The material encompasses formal and informal leadership, a guide to formulate a personal definition of leadership, and an introduction to the Great Man and Trait theories.

Chapter Five: Paradigms of Leadership
As Part Two is designed to help the reader evolve her/his own leadership style, this chapter introduces the reader to some of the fundamental theories of leadership. By becoming conversant with some of the existing paradigms of leadership, the reader would be able to assess her/his SWOT (strengths, weaknesses, opportunities and threats) in order to harness her/his personality traits and abilities for good leadership.

Chapter Six: Developing Leadership Core Competence
This chapter weaves self-assessment, public speaking skills, knowledgebase expansion for sustainable good degree of leadership performance, recognition of the needs of others and ethics to help the reader develop core competences for democratic leadership personality. This part of the book draws the conclusion that a combination of democracy and leadership opens up to a good life saturated by human dignity.

PART THREE: DEMOCRACY AND LEADERSHIP COMBINED

Chapter Seven: Linking Democracy and Leadership
Here the authors combine important aspects of democracy and leadership and suggest a number of actions which may be taken to realize applicable ideas in the previous chapters for our daily lives.

DEMOCRACY AND LEADERSHIP: A WAY OF LIFE

Odd Ragnar Hunnes

Michael Flowers

Flowers Publications
Flowers School of Technology and Management
Germany • United Kingdom

Hunnes, Odd Ragnar; Flowers, Michael
Leadership and Democracy: a way of life | Odd Ragnar Hunnes, Michael
Flowers

ISBN-13: 978-1481961875 | ISBN-10: 148196187X

Democracy, Empowerment, Human Dignity, Human Rights, Leadership,
Motivation, Strategic Leadership.

Printed in the United States of America

This book delivers principles and strategies that the authors individually
believe and recommend to readers. Notwithstanding, it is not a guarantee that
perusal of material in this book will by all means lead to your democratic
leadership excellence in your community. You acknowledge the fact that your
experience and achievement depend on a multiplicity of factors which include
(but are not limited to) your idiosyncrasies, capacities and the socio-economic
realities of your society, which are unknown to the authors.

www.flowers.ac

CONTENTS

ABOUT THE
AUTHORS

Odd Ragnar Hunnes
is a professor of Geography teaching within the teacher education at Volda University College in Norway. For more than thirty years he has worked with education as an administrator, leader, researcher and teacher and has had extensive contact with Africa in these capacities. His published works include his co-editorship of *Learning Democracy: A Resource Book* available for free at:
http://www.hivolda.no/nyn/andre/democracy-in-teacher-training-1/a-resource-book.

Michael Flowers
is a Chartered Engineer, strategist, consultant, researcher and trainer at the Flowers School of Technology and Management in Germany, the UK and Ghana. His focus has been leadership, innovation, entrepreneurship, sustainable development, strategic visioning, self-enrichment, appropriate (intermediate) technology for developing countries, and education. An inventor, his publishing portfolio includes self-development based textbooks such as Creative Writing and Authorpreneurship, and The Moneymaking Code, and scholarly articles.

PART ONE

DEMOCRACY

Chapter 1

SO WHAT IS DEMOCRACY?

'It is an indisputable fact that democracy, along with a handful of other concerns such as health, development and peace, has become one of the core and foremost preoccupations of the people of the world today. All over the world, millions of men and women are clamouring for it, ready to consent enormous sacrifices of sweat, tears and blood, up to and including death, to secure it. This is the measure of the value of democracy to civilized mankind.' — Afrifa Githonga

1.1 The what and how in government

In general, governments exist to secure order, equality and freedom in a society and to supply certain public goods and services in the same. The main purpose of order is to preserve life and property, if necessary by the use of force. The Human Development Report (HDR) claims that 'when order breaks down in a country, poor people usually suffer first and most' (UN 2002: 6), indicating an important link between order and equality. Equality may be reached through redistribution of wealth and securing a minimum of human welfare, and a main question of debate is how to define equality and how to fund the provision of it. Both order and equality will most certainly reduce the individual freedom of the citizens. Therefore, striking a good balance between order, equality and freedom is a fundamental and continuous challenge for any government. Public goods and services may be physical infrastructure (clean water, sewage, roads and the like), health services and education,

The substantive part of government

and the relevant political debate runs along the line of how much of which goods the government should provide for and what should be left for the private sector to cater for. That which is mentioned so far may be called the substantive part of government, or *what* the government tries to do (Janda et al 1993).

The
procedural
part of
government

The procedural (or formal) part of government focuses on *how* government tries to do what it wants to do. To conclude on such matters (both what to do and how to do it), decisions have to be made. A main activity in government, therefore, is decision making. Democracy offers a set of normative principles for how government, actually any ruling body, ought to make decisions (ibid). The aim of this chapter is to give an overview over democratic principles and the values and the culture that go with it.

1.2 Some central aspects on democracy

Democracy
is a relati-
vely new
concept in
history

Starting with the philosophers and practices of the city states of ancient Greece and reinforced by the assumption that 'all men are created equal', it has been a long and difficult process to reach universal suffrage and citizens' participation in decision making in societies. Shutt observes that in this perspective it is fair to say that the Western world has been pioneering the establishment of common citizenship and he continues to write: 'Seen from the perspective of human history [...] the idea of popular democracy based on mass enfranchisement is still relatively new' (201: 146).

Government
of, by and
for the
people

Abraham Lincoln in his Gettisburg address defined democracy as government of, by and for the people, a definition that has been cited often since. *Of* the people should indicate that the government is not alien to the peoples' way of life; it is in accordance with the values, attitudes and habits of the people, in short: the people's culture. This is commonly expressed in the country's constitution. *By* the people may mean the rule of law, as the law is accepted by the ruled ones. Rule of law should be combined with the people's possibility to decide who should make decisions and also influence the decisions that are made. Participation is a key concept in this connection. *For* the people means that the people are the ones who should benefit from the government's decisions, be it in material, spiritual, psychological, social or in other ways (Githonga 1987).

1.2.1 Rule of law

The procedural part of government in a democracy is usually described in the constitution of the country and in additional laws, rules and regulations. A fundamental aspect of the rule of law is that there are procedures and regulations concerning how decisions should be made, who should be given power to act on behalf of government and how this power should be handed over to others. Rule of law also implies that the content of the laws, rules and regulations is generally known and everybody, the government as well as the citizen, is obliged to live by them. Therefore an important part of developing democracy in a country is to write the needed or wanted changes into 'the law' of that society and to follow this up through unbiased enforcement.

Procedures for decision making

In addition to the laws internal to a country, there are international conventions and declarations that have a substantial influence on governance and the way of life in most countries. A well known example is the UN's Universal Declaration of Human Rights (DHR), which most countries have ratified. The mere existence of DHR is a continuous reminder to legislation and performance by governments worldwide. It is also very effectively used as a

International conventions

tool for human right's organizations to pressure governments to follow suit.

1.2.2 A matter of culture – a matter of daily life

The core:
Human
dignity

The underlying value of democracy is human dignity[1]. Human dignity implies that a person deserves respect by self and others, develops the ability and is given the opportunity to participate in community life. This respect is mainly shown through the intention of meeting the set of psychological, spiritual, social and material needs every human being has. Parts of these needs imply ability to influence own destiny through having a say in how decisions should be made as well as the material content of the decisions. The Human Development Report underlines the importance of this by claiming that the freedom to express one's views and participate in decision making are just as important for human development as being able to read or enjoy good health (UN 2002). Masolo states that democracy is 'an attitude because it is a way of doing things that is dependent upon how we regard ourselves, our abilities and those of others' (1987: 24). Consequently, on the individual level, democracy is also a matter of identity, a matter of who we are. Therefore, respecting democracy when this suits our own ends and disregarding it when it seems to be to own disadvantage, is a violation to own identity and to the idea of democracy. On the society level, democracy is also a matter of culture and even the social 'climate' (Pateman 1970).

A transfor-
mation is
needed

In his paper "'We Want Change": Transition or Transformation?' Chirwa (1998) maintains that countries need to realize a *transformation* to democracy and not limit the process of democratization to a *transition*. While transition only shows on the surface, for instance through established procedures and institutions, a transformation

---

[1] See the chapter 2 for more on human dignity

18

goes deeper and is characterized by a change in culture with the ideas, values, attitudes and practices that are associated with this culture. A transformation therefore is about a social process and a political practice which are founded on a moral imperative. This moral imperative is associated with human dignity and the indigenous culture of the particular society.

As democracy is a matter of culture, identity and human dignity it also reads: a matter of life. The moral imperative is not only about decision making in different institutions, important as that certainly is. It is about all aspects of life; at work and during leisure time, in public and private. In short: in our daily life.

1.3   Important features

The Human Development Report 2002 presents some important features for democracy as a mode of government. It states that political and civil freedoms allowing citizens to think, speak and act as participants in decision making are obvious assets of democracy compared to other systems. Transparency makes it possible for the citizens to hold government accountable and this may help protect people from economic and political catastrophes such as famines and descents into chaos. Even so, in its review on the literature on democracy and economic growth, the report points out that there are few consistent patterns to be found worldwide. Empirical studies are largely inconclusive. However, there seem to be some robust findings. One of them is that at all income levels, fertility rates are significantly lower in democracies. This may be interpreted as a sign of optimism and improved human welfare (Mamdani 1974, Hesselberg & Engh 1998).

Democracy holds the government accountable

Furthermore there seems to be certain relationships between economic performance and democratic governance. The HDR (UN 2002: 56) reports that:

Democracy shows economic performance 'in the middle'

- While the economic performance of dictatorships varies from terrible to excellent, democracies tend to cluster in the middle.

- The fastest growing countries have typically been dictatorships, but no democracy has ever performed as badly as the worst dictatorships. The same is true for poverty reduction. Thus democracy appears to prevent the worst outcomes, even if it does not guarantee the best ones.

- Middle-income countries have been more likely than poor or rich countries to move from dictatorships to democracies

- There is also evidence that reversions to authoritarianism are likely in economic downturns, but it is not clear [...] whether bad economic performance causes democracies to fall or whether democracies about to fall exhibit bad performance.

Democracy is associa-ted with political stability

Democracies seem to contribute to political stability since they provide open space for political opposition and handovers of power. In its overview the HDR 2002 illustrates this argument by pointing to the time period between 1950 and 1990. In this period riots and demonstrations were more common in democracies, but more destabilizing in dictatorships. Moreover, wars were more frequent in non-democratic regimes and had much higher economic costs compared to democracies.

Finally the report maintains that democratic governance can trigger 'a virtuous cycle of development' since political freedom empowers people to take responsibility and influence decisions through discussion. Consequently, the report presents the following strategy for human development: 'For politics and political institutions to promote human development and safeguard the freedom and dignity of all people, democracy must widen and deepen' (UN 2001: 1).

Kamwendo (1998) points out that since language touches on the soul and identity of any society it is also an important aspect of the process of democratization of a country. Broch-Utne (2000: 149) describes language as 'culture expressing itself in sound' a statement that underscores the link between language and democracy. Here the use of the vernacular as the language of instruction in schools and the language of information and debate in politics is very much in focus. Chauma, Kholowa and Holby write that 'Success stories indicate that learners perform better when the mother tongue is the medium of instruction' (2007: 146). Similarly they claim that democratic values are more easily acquired when they are communicated in the vernacular: 'Mother tongue literacy can promote understanding of democratic values, a sense of identity as well as self esteem. Lack of communication with the masses in a language that they understand has been a main cause of hindrance to creating a democratic culture' (ibid: 152-153). At the same time, we know that in most African countries the citizens belong to different ethnic groups and therefore have different languages as their mother tongue. Consequently they need a common language on the state level in order to communicate efficiently and for democracy to prosper. Such common languages may be Kiswahili, Hausa, English, French etc. The relationship between language and democracy is a fundamental one and needs to be further elaborated upon, politically as well as academically.

Democracy links to language

1.4   Dimensions and foundations of democracy

In his paper 'The meaning and foundations of democracy'

Afrifa Githonga (1987) points out three dimensions and three foundations of democracy[2]. There are the abstract, the practical and the concrete dimension, while the foundations are the infrastructure, the technostructure and the superstructure. This is tentatively illustrated in figure 1.

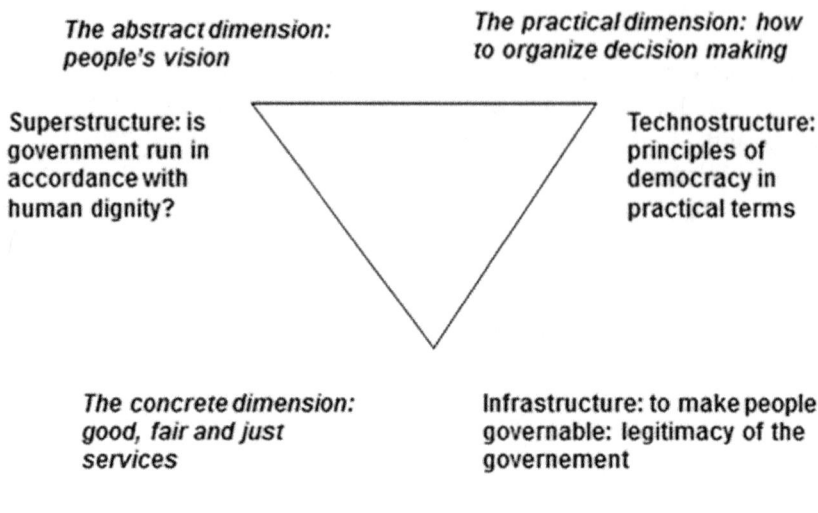

The abstract dimension: people's vision

The practical dimension: how to organize decision making

Superstructure: is government run in accordance with human dignity?

Technostructure: principles of democracy in practical terms

The concrete dimension: good, fair and just services

Infrastructure: to make people governable: legitimacy of the governement

Figure 1: The dimensions and foundations of democracy.

People's vision

The abstract dimension exists in the imagination of men and women. It is an intellectual creation, a mental model of what is possible within given frameworks. In its abstract dimension democracy is therefore a vision, a dream. A democratic system is one which has its roots in the people's culture (ideas, values, attitudes and practice) and therefore is not foreign to people's ideals. It is rather created in the particular people's image, thus being representative of the people that is being governed and their vision of their society.

---

[2] The following part of the present chapter draws heavily on Githonga's paper in structure, points made and wording used.

The practical dimension exists in the ways and means of men and women, in short: how things are done in a particular society. This dimension of democracy is about how the vision, the ideas and ideals are transformed into reality. It is mainly the question of how to organize decision making. Janda et al (1993: 37) point to three basic questions that need to be addressed in this connection:

To transform the vision into reality

- Who should participate in decision making?
- How much should each participant's preferences count in voting?
- How many voters are needed to reach a decision?

The fundamental principle in this context should be political equity, which means equal rights and equal responsibilities for citizens. This principle is often illustrated by the slogan 'one person, one vote'.

Political equity

It is obvious that decision making must be organized, or structured. There should be some kind of division of labour, division of responsibilities and division of rights. This is what is commonly called the 'separation of powers' in government, where checks and balances are built into the structures, securing a balance of power between the different branches and different institutions of government. A deep wisdom is expressed in the phrase that 'no person should be accuser, judge and executioner all in one'. The separation of powers also leads to the matter of sharing out work for greater operational efficiency, creating institutions which have their specialized tasks within government. And traditionally the assembly of the representatives of the people has the supreme authority and all the other institutions of government are subordinate to it.

The separation of powers is fundamental

The concrete dimension exists in the experience of men and women and concerns to what degree they find the government delivering good, fair and just services in their everyday life. Lip service to principles and procedures is not good enough. The success of a democracy is measured by what it delivers of order, equality, freedom and public goods and services in the manner and magnitude the people needs and wishes. 'The proof of the pudding is the eating' and the proof of the democracy shows through the ability to deliver good benefits to 'the people'. In this context a statement by Masolo (1987: 25) should be noted: 'what is to be considered as good rests with those that are governed'.

Does the government deliver good, fair and just services?

The first foundation to be mentioned is *the superstructure of democracy* and this is to be found in the values, beliefs, attitudes and practices of the people. 'And since the people must govern together, collectively, there is no way they can do so without a minimum of respect for one another, without according each other the right to human dignity…' (Githonga 1987: 22).

The acid test: Is government run in accordance with human dignity?

The technostructure of democracy concerns principles of democracy in practical terms. The following set of principles, or characteristics of a sound democracy, is compiled mainly on the basis of HDR (UN 2002: 51) and Chidam'modzi (1999: 95):

Principles of democracy in practical terms

- People's human rights and fundamental freedoms are respected, allowing them to live with dignity, which means that citizens are treated as rational, morally sensitive and active people.
- Consent of the governed is the basis of the government's authority.
- Relations between citizens and government are characterized by freedom and responsibility.

- People have a say in decisions that affect their lives for example through free and fair elections at regular intervals and consultations on specific issues.
- People can hold decision makers accountable based on an ample access to relevant information.
- The government maintains impartial systems of justice and rule by law.
- Inclusive and fair procedures, institutions and practices govern social interactions.
- Women are equal partners with men in private and public spheres of life and decision making.
- People are free from discrimination based on race, ethnicity, class, religion, gender or any other attribute.
- There is tolerance of dissident or opposing views and peaceful resolution of conflicts.
- Economic and social policies are responsive to people's needs and aspirations.
- Economic and social policies aim at eradicating poverty and expanding the choices that all people have in their lives.
- The needs of future generations are reflected in current policies.

Surely this list could be made longer, but making it shorter may be a better idea. Githonga seems to suggest that the principles of the technostructure of democracy may be summed up as openness, simplicity and clarity (1987: 20):

Charac-teristics:
- openness
- simplicity
- clarity

1. The system should be open.
2. The operational mechanisms should be simple.
3. The institutional role structure should be clear.

The last foundation of democracy is *the infrastructure of democracy* which is about making people governable. Put differently, this is about the legitimacy of the government. In this connection he stresses the economy. The system of

*To make
people
governable:
legitimacy
of the
government*

production, distribution and consumption of material goods and services must cater for the so-called basic human needs in order to make people willing and able to be governed according to democratic principles. In addition come the cultural aspects that also contribute to shape people's motivation and ability for governance.

1.5 Dilemmas

Having described the dimensions and foundations of democracy, it is important to look at some of the dilemmas that become evident once the ideas and ideals are transformed into practical action.

1.5.1 A tremendous social and political experiment

*Democra-
tic ideals:
capable of
shooting
democracy
in the foot*

Plato observed that democracy cannot guarantee good governance because it depends on the whims of the masses and according to him the masses are the least knowledgeable. Thus democracy may encourage opportunistic leadership, prioritizing issues and making decisions that are popular with voters rather than necessary for the people. Also, because of its emphasis on liberty, every individual may feel free to do as s/he likes, disregarding possible negative consequences of one's actions. 'In short, democratic ideals are capable of shooting democracy in the foot' (Chidam'modzi 1999: 95).

Obviously there is a need for a minimum of knowledge, moral and personal integrity among the participants in decision making. However, to find out if or when people have this minimum competence seems to be an impossible task. Thus democracy actually comes out as a tremendous social and political experiment depending on people's decision making competence. There are three mechanisms that may help to safeguard against negative effects of this experiment. First is the hope and belief that people rise to match the responsibilities that come with the freedom and the rights of democracy. Second is the institutional separation of powers in the government with the checks and balances that come with it. Third is the continuous capacity building in democracy aimed at every society and every citizen. In this connection the education system and the media are important tools for information and communication.

Some safeguards

1.5.2 Legitimacy and representation

Legitimacy of a government is very much depending on the degree of human welfare the citizens experience. Therefore, Janda et al (1993: 44) point out that 'Governments must have means for determining what the people want, as well as some means for translating those wants into acceptable decisions. In other words, democratic government requires institutional mechanisms - established procedures and organizations - to translate public opinion into government policy to be responsive.' If we were to be true to the very idea of democracy, which actually means 'popular power', this should be done through direct rule. But in most societies the complexity and multitude of cases that have to be decided upon, makes it impractical if not impossible for citizens to participate to a full extent. The usual solution to this problem is for the citizens to elect some persons to act on their behalf. The Nigeria born political scientist Claude Ake claims that this solution 'replaces government by the people with government by the consent of the people' (2003: 10). He argues that 'representative democracy' is a contradiction in terms and the main reason for why it is accepted by privileged people in society is that representative democracy makes it possible for them to maintain their privileges and dominate the politics of the land. Anyhow, the major challenge is to find persons who are really representative of the citizens in the kinds of cases that need acting upon. This challenge grows larger as it is taken into account that persons who in the beginning very well may be representative of 'the man in the street',

What do people want?

Represen-
tatives
become
professional
decision
makers

through time build their own capacity in decision making: they become to a lesser or larger degree professional decision makers, in other words: professional politicians. These are able to devote more time and effort to politics and have access to more information than the people they are elected to represent. Naturally it is very difficult to determine what kind of conclusions the average citizen would arrive at providing s/he had access to the same amount of time and information as their representative(s) enjoy. To complicate matters, in a representative democracy the citizens get a substantial portion of their information from their elected politicians, usually delivered through the media. This of course makes the citizens prone to manipulation by their representative(s). Transparency, ample access to information and possibilities for two way communication between represented and representative seem to be important measures in an effort to balance this challenge.

The
politician
has double
roles:
represent-
tative and
leader

To complicate matters even more, the politicians are often expected to be representatives of 'the average citizen' and to be visionary and communicative leaders at the same time. With the responsibility of being visionary comes the need to assess matters in a long time perspective. This may implicate the need to abstain from enjoying short term benefits for the favour of possible or probable long term benefits.

In the discussion of the relationship between represented and representatives it is also relevant to point at the danger of the representatives using their position to patronage the citizens. Shutt claims that 'One of the most corrupting features of contemporary Western democracy is the enormous power of patronage typically placed in the hands of high officials' (2001: 158). Obviously the highest official is the party leader, in African context this frequently also is the party founder. In a newspaper interview[3], political scientist Jacob Jimu comments on the situation in Malawi: 'We have political parties that are not founded on any principles but the personality of the party founder.' He then continues to explain how the tradition of the 'Big Man' syndrome is perpetuated into the political party machinery. The Big Man to a large degree determines the party's policies and is himself the party's 'communication strategy'. He sees to it that people who are loyal to him / the party are rewarded accordingly. The feature of hand outs at political rallies is an often mentioned example of how this works on the grass-root level. So a patron – client relationship between the leader and the followers is often established and kept alive as 'everyone dances to his tune'. Therefore, the challenge to play down 'personality politics' and strengthen 'issue-based politics' is important to address. This is the case not only in Africa since in many countries political parties in their election campaigns seem to emphasize the personality of their candidates to a larger degree than their policies.

The possibility of patron – client relationship

In order for representative democracy to function well, the representative's attitude to the job is probably the most important. In essence, politics is about power and the representatives are elected to exercise some kind of power. It is therefore crucial that this power is exercised on behalf of the citizens and to their fair benefit rather than to the politician's own benefit. Therefore Shutt (2001) points out that it is important to nominate and elect politicians who are motivated by public service rather than personal ambition and acquisitiveness. Society needs politicians who identify with the view that holding office is more a duty than a privilege. This need is clearly illustrated by the fact that the term 'politician' in the Malawian language Chichewa actually means 'someone who plays tricks on people'.

Power should be exercised to the benefit of the citizens

Holding office should be a duty rather than a privilege

---

[3] The interview appears 20.07.2003 in the Weekend Nation (Malawi) and the headline reads: 'Personality politics degrades democracy'

1.5.3 Considerations concerning decision making

Majority rule – the main principle

It is a common notion that in a group of decision makers, the majority generally should have its way. This is what usually is named 'majority rule'. However, there are some reasons for holding a consequent majority rule back, and below the following examples are touched upon: minority rights, low voter turn-out, efficient administration and judiciary and decisions that have long term consequences.

Minority rights – human rights

There are some rights that everybody is entitled to, sometimes referred to as minority rights. These rights should not be run over by a majority vote. Most people will agree that minority rights are for instance freedom of expression, freedom of assembly and freedom of religion. We know these as fundamental human rights[4]. Opinion may differ on what else belongs to the category of minority rights. The following example may illustrate this. In Malawian context 'freedom of dress' is often mentioned as an example among civil liberties (for instance Chirwa 1998) demonstrating a reaction to the strict dress code that was imposed on civil society by the Banda regime (1961 – 1994). This raises the question whether freedom of dress should be classified as a minority right. Opinion may also differ concerning to what extent minority rights may be executed in a society. Freedom of expression gives a person the right to voice her/his opinion. Even so, this does certainly not imply the right to express anything on one's mind, including insulting or throwing dubious suspicion on somebody else. A line has to be drawn somewhere, and the question of where to draw it is just as important as it is difficult.

Majority rule also faces a dilemma in instances when there is little voter turn-out in an election. What is the legitimacy

---

[4] See The Universal Declaration of Human Rights:
http://www.un.org/en/documents/udhr/

of decisions made by a majority established through a low turn-out of voters? It is difficult to make general statements on this question. It has to be dealt with in each case individually and calls for thorough consideration and wisdom. Nevertheless, it also underlines every citizen's responsibility to exercise one's right to vote.

Low voter turn-out

In any government there are a vast number of decisions that need to be made. The principle of separation of powers in government implies that there are some types of decisions that should be withdrawn from the political scene. Examples may be decisions within the judicial and administrative parts of government, where laws, rules and procedures are there to guide the decision makers. Impartiality, efficiency and the spread of influence and power are major gains in this respect.

Decisions made by the administration and the judiciary

Most constitutions have regulations that imply that 50% of the votes are not enough to change it. Often 2/3 or more of the votes are necessary. In some cases a change in a country's constitution also needs to be backed by a sufficient majority of the votes from two consecutive elections to the national assembly. This is for example the case for the constitution of Norway. Similar rules may be written into the constitution of Non Governmental Organizations (NGOs), businesses and the like. The motive behind this is that constitutions should be relatively stable and not subject to changes based on the whims of people or short time pressure groups. Similar restrictions on majority rule may be put on different types of decisions that have long lasting consequences in any country, municipality or organization that is run according to democratic principles.

Decisions with long term consequences

1.6 Civil society and decision making processes

Vehicles for participa-tion

Parallel with the model of majority rule runs the pluralist model which interprets government by the people as a system operating through competing interest groups. Political parties and trade unions have traditionally been the main instruments for people's participation in politics. But during the last few decades, NGOs and other organizations in civil society have increased their influence in this respect. Membership in different types of organizations may vary from time to time, reflecting different trends in society. It is therefore important to have a wide variety of vehicles for people's participation in decision making, offering opportunities for different people to influence decisions they find important. So best possible access to decision making processes and influential organizations for all, is an important ideal in a democracy. Still, in the real world, we know that people have uneven access to interest groups and uneven resources to participate in them. In addition, the influence such a group may have, depends heavily on the resources it has at its disposal. A problem in point is how people with money or other important resources may secure for themselves undue influence on the agenda as well as the content of concrete political decisions. Shutt (2001) claims that in order to enhance the quality of democracy in the Western world and elsewhere, restricting the influence of money interests is the one most important action to take. Alongside restrictions, he writes that transparency concerning the funding of political parties and political activities is absolutely necessary.

Challenge: uneven access

Important to restrict the influence of money

1.7 Democracy and school

Democracy depends on education

John Dewey states that democracy is devoted to education and this is so because 'a government resting upon popular suffrage cannot be successful unless those who elect and who obey their governors are educated' (1966: 87). Clearly, to have a genuine democracy, citizens must have a minimum of general understanding of society combined with more specific knowledge of the matters to be decided upon and on how to make decisions. This kind of knowledge does not come by itself, it needs to be taught. The teaching may take place in different institutions in society, for instance in homes, religious and social groups and schools. In the following, schools will be focused.

It goes without saying that schools need to give the students a good cognitive understanding of the term democracy. The students need to grapple with the concept, looking at it from different angles, familiarizing themselves with the obvious strengths of democracy as well as the many dilemmas. Strange as it may seem, this probably is the easier part of the necessary democracy learning, mainly because it concerns learning *about* democracy. In essence this is a theoretical approach to the concept which certainly must be taken seriously. Even so, the most important, difficult and time consuming part is the learning *for* democracy. This learning for democracy has several important aspects that need to be addressed.

*Learning **about** democracy is easier than learning **for** democracy*

One aspect is the wide variety that constitutes the value base of democracy. This needs not only to be understood intellectually, but also to be learned in such a way that these values become part of the learners' own values, part of their identity. The main goal is that the learners internalize the values, beliefs, attitudes and practices of human dignity, so that human dignity becomes an important part of the learners' personal and fundamental values. If the teacher limits this teaching to talking, explaining and reading about these values, s/he will fail. These values have to show in the teacher's own attitudes and practices. This means for instance treating the students not like objects, but with respect, care and love. It also means to help students build their confidence so that they dare trust their own judgment, to voice their opinions, respect other people's opinion and yield to the better argument. In these ways the teacher may create a relaxed and secure atmosphere conducive to learning about and for democracy as well as other subjects.

The value base must be interna-lized

The teacher must treat students with respect

Another aspect is the practice of democratic procedures in the schools. MacJessie-Mbewe (1999: 29) states that 'Teachers, students, school administrators, and other participants in the educational system must understand what constitutes democracy and how it can be applied in educational institutions'. Understanding is not enough. Therefore teachers and administrators need to find ways to practice democracy in their own institution. The teachers need to introduce their students to participation in decision making concerning activities in school. This may be about teaching methods and activities in the classroom. It may be about deciding on codes of conduct, rules and regulations for the everyday life in the school itself. It is definitely about creating situations where the students are consulted, starting with decisions of limited consequences for the younger students and escalating as the students' maturity develop. Examples may be democratic decision making about a field trip and the running of a student enterprise (see Tafjord 2007).

Find ways to practice democracy

Democratic attitudes and procedures are important for the everyday life in the school itself and at the same time they point beyond school. MacJessie-Mbewe writes that 'Our students should learn, while still in school, the democratic behaviour of being able to negotiate, by listening to and valuing the views of others, so that they fit easily into the larger democratic society in which they will live after school' (1999: 25). Therefore it is also an important challenge for schools to motivate students to participate in elections and other democratic procedures for decision making and problem solving. The students should also learn how decisions are made through voting, how to administer a debate in such a way that everybody who is entitled to speak, is allowed to do so and more of that kind. Naturally the schools should not neglect to teach their students the technicalities of democracy.

The technicali-ties of democracy must be learned

Teaching democracy and developing a democratic culture

is a long process, a deep commitment to the principles of democracy must be adopted. It is not sufficient for the students to learn to know the *word* democracy they need to know the *concept*. It is a question of developing democracy as a habit and a common understanding and sense of common responsibility: a spirit of commonness (Midtgard & Rash 2004). This takes time and patience to foster. The school is in a unique position to make a positive difference in this respect.

1.8   Democracy grows in a combination of expansion and inclusion

In this chapter it is pointed out that democracy is not only a matter of governance. It is also a matter of people's shared values, beliefs, attitudes, standards, morals, customs, habits and knowledge. In short: democracy is also a matter of culture.

Hand in hand democratic governance and culture should be nurtured in processes of interaction where both individual and social perspectives are included. Expansion and inclusion are key words for these processes. Expansion to all levels and areas of community life and inclusion of every individual and group therein. As Rutto & Njoroge explain: 'There is need […] to develop a conception of democracy […] that goes beyond the political domain. There is need to take democratic discourse to homes, schools, churches and offices of public administrators. In this way, the context of the growth of democratic attitudes, abilities and culture is enlarged' (2001: 60).

Democracy should be practised in a widening range of contexts

Study questions for Chapter 1

1. Explain the difference between the substantive and the procedural parts of government.
2. Explain the meaning of the statement that democracy is government of, by and for the people.
3. Name some of the important advantages of democracy compared to other modes of government.
4. Explain the dimensions and foundations of democracy.
5. In this chapter democracy is claimed to be a tremendous social and political experiment. Which mechanisms may help to safeguard against possible negative effects of this experiment?
6. What are the advantages and disadvantages of representative democracy?
7. Majority rule is a main principle in democracy. Discuss some reasonable limitations to majority rule.
8. What is the main difference between *learning about democracy* and *learning for democracy*? Explain why the latter is considered to be more difficult.
9. Why should democracy be practiced in schools?

References

Ake, C (2003): *The Feasibility of Democracy in Africa.* Oxford: African Books Collective.

Broch-Utne, B (2002): *Whose Education for All? The Recolinization of the African Mind.* New York & London: Falmer Press.

Chauma, A, F. Kholowa and K.N Holby (2007): 'Promoting the Use of Mother Tongue in Education – a Case for Democracy' In Hunnes O.R and M.N Chilambo: *Learning Democracy. A resource book.* Balaka: Montfort Media. May be found on the internet: http://www.hivolda.no/democracy.

Chidam'modzi, H.F (1999): 'Democracy and tradition in Malawi'. In Chimombo, M. *Lessons in Hope: Education for Democracy in Malawi, Past, Present, Future.* Zomba: National Chancellor College Publications.

Chirwa, C.W (1998): '"We Want Change": Transition or Transformation?' In Tsoka M and C. Mikey, *Bwalo. A forum for social development*, Issue 2. Zomba: University of Malawi.

Dewey, J (1966): *Democracy and education.* New York: The Free Press. A Division of Macmillan Publishing Co.

Githonga, A.K (1995): 'The meaning and foundations of democracy.' In Oyugi, W. O and A. K Githonga (eds.), *Democratic theory and practice in Africa.* Nairobi: East African Education Publishers.

Hesselberg, J and I.E Engh (1998): 'Befolkningsspørsmålet'. In Hesselberg, J (ed.), *Utviklingsgeografi.* Oslo: Tano Aschehoug.

Janda, K, J.F. Berry and J. Goldman (1993): *The challenge of democracy. Government in America.* Boston: Houghton Mifflin Company.

Kamwendo, G.H (1998): 'Democracy and Language Policy Reforms in Malawi: 1994 – 1997'. In Tsoka, M and C. Mikey, *Bwalo. A forum for social development*, Issue 2. Zomba: University of Malawi.

MacJessie-Mbewe, S.L.W. (1999): 'Power vs. authority in the democratic Malawian classroom.' In Chimombo, M *Lessons in Hope: Education for Democracy in Malawi, Past, Present, Future.* Zomba: National Chancellor

College Publications.

Mamdani, M (1974): 'The Myth of Population Control: Family, Caste and Class in an Indian Village'. New York, London: Monthly's Review Press.

Masolo, D.A (1987): 'Ideological Dogmatism and the Values of Democracy'. In Oyugi, W.O and A.K Githonga (ed): *Democratic theory and practice in Africa*. Nairobi: East African Education Publishers.

Moto, F (1998): 'Domesticating the Definition of Democracy'. In Tsoka, M and C. Mikey, *Bwalo. A forum for social development*, Issue 2. Zomba: University of Malawi.

Pateman, C (1970): *Participation and democratic theory*. London: Cambridge University Press.

Rutto, S. K and G. K Njoroge (2001): *The democratization process in Africa* Nairobi: Quest & Insight.

Shutt, H (2001): *A New Democracy. Alternatives to a bankrupt world order*. London: Zed Books Ltd.

Tafjord, B (2007): 'Entrepreneurship and Democracy' In Hunnes O.R and M.N Chilambo: *Learning Democracy. A resource book*. Balaka: Montfort Media. May be found on the internet: http://www.hivolda.no/democracy.

UN (2002): *Human Development Report 2002. Deepening democracy in a fragmented world*. Oxford, New York: Oxford University Press.

Chapter 2

HUMAN DIGNITY — THE CORE VALUE OF DEMOCRACY

'*... the debate and the promotion of democracy in Africa is not complete without reference to the dignity of the African people.*' — Rutto & Njoroge

Man is a special being, and this specialty gives her/him a distinguished dignity. This dignity has a huge potential in many ways. Martin Luther King jr. explained his fight against racial segregation in the US with statements to the effect that this policy was an attack on human dignity in general (Washington 1991, Phillips 1998). The main point is that the way society is organized should reflect how we fundamentally view the human being and in this context dignity is essential. The aim of this chapter is therefore to present the concept of human dignity as a core value for any society that strives to promote wellbeing for its members. With the many properties that a democracy has[5], this presentation implicitly argues that human dignity is the founding value upon which everything within democracy is built.

Man – a special being

---

[5] See Chapter 1 for a presentation of some important properties of democracy.

2.1 Why *human* dignity?

The base for human dignity may be the belief or conviction that the human being is created by God to have communion with other humans and God, and to manage the world on God's behalf. This is the view held within Christianity, Islam and Judaism. In addition, Christianity and Judaism teach that the human being is created in God's image.

Man is spiritual, has a conscience and is able to reason

It may also be argued that man has a special capacity for reason and conscience that puts her/him on a level of her/his own among all beings, as it is coined in the Universal Declaration of Human Rights of 1948, Article 1:

'All human beings are born free and equal in dignity and rights. They are endowed with reason and conscience and should act towards one another in a spirit of brotherhood.'

Human life – an obvious worth

Rutto & Njoroge write: 'To assign dignity to human life, so to speak, implies to value human life; it is to recognize human life as precious and possessing an obvious worth.' (2001: 1).

There may be scores of other reasons, but the three mentioned above should be sufficient as a starting point for this chapter: the human being is a special species that deserves a special dignity.

2.2 Some aspects of human dignity

2.2.1 Respect

Human dignity implies that a person deserves respect by self and others. This respect is mainly shown through the intention of meeting the set of psychological, spiritual, social and material needs every human being has. So being respected means acknowledgement of legitimate needs for all this: to develop one's talents, to practice one's religion, to be an active part of a social entity, to cover one's needs for food, drink, clothing, shelter etc. In addition comes that the needs also mean ability to influence one's own destiny through having a say in how decisions that influence one's life should be made as well as in the material content of such decisions. This side of respect implies recognizing the individual as a subject rather than an object of forces that shape one's life. To regard the other as a subject is a way of confirming her/him as having the ability to contribute to her/his own development, rather than just being a victim of external forces. Several Human Development Reports underline the importance of this by claiming that the freedom to express one's views and participate in decision making, in short: empowerment, are just as important for human development as being able to read or enjoy good health (UN 1993, 2000, 2002, 2004, 2005, 2006, 2007/2008, 2009, 2010).

Acknow-ledgement of legitimate needs

See the individual as a subject

To find out what all this actually means, we need to be actively seeing and actively listening[6]. Here a distinction between looking and seeing, hearing and listening should be made. Looking and hearing merely means to register impulses that come from a sender and are received through eye and ear. Active seeing and active listening means trying to find out what the other person wants/tries to communicate and then give relevant feed-back to this. Active seeing and listening are focused on the sender's

Active listening and active seeing

---

[6] See more about active listening in chapter 6

intended message and relates to this. It is not a question of agreeing with the other person but of respecting her/him.

2.2.2 Reciprocity

Being respected means having the right to be listened to as well as the right to speak. In essence, this is what dialogue is about. The Russian language philosopher Bakhtin claims that life is dialogical in nature and that the human being can only understand herself/himself in relation to *the other* (Dysthe 1999). The Norwegian philosopher Fløistad goes along with this as he writes that it is in relation to *the other* the individual best can acknowledge and become the real self (Fløistad 1996). This is sometimes referred to as using each other as a mirror into which we look in order to know ourselves. The number one point for this 'mirror' is to see and the second is to give feed-back and it is amazing to note how important it is for a person's self-esteem to be 'seen' and be given feed-back from *the others*.

Dialogue – a way of living

True dialogue involves equal partners and creates fellowship with potential to find solutions that work well for society, for the common good. It is characterised by truth, frankness, sincerity, earnestness, fairness and the like. And it yields to the better argument. Some even take this to be the normative core of democracy (Solhaug and Børhaug 2012).

Reciprocity is not only about words, it is also about action. I observed the text on a poster in a public toilet once: 'Please leave this toilet in the same state as you would like to find it'. It is a very concrete example of the Golden Rule: 'Do unto others as you would like others to do unto you.'

It is about words – and acts

Among the many features concerning reciprocity that additionally could be mentioned, just one has been picked for this presentation: trust. My home country is Norway and for a number of years Norway has been doing very well in the UN's Human Development Index as this has been reported in several Human Development Reports. Our living standards are good, and many have wondered why this is so. The country is very fortunate with plenty of natural resources: the ocean has fish, abundant precipitation is turned into hydro-electric power and since the latter part of the 1960s: petroleum (oil and gas). Now, there are a number of African countries that are affluent in natural resources. So what is there to explain the difference in human welfare? There is a lot of literature where the question of why development in Africa is lagging behind has been analysed. The list of explanations is long and the legacy of colonization, bad governance, cancerous corruption and (lately) a culture of dependency (Maathai 2009) are frequently mentioned. Among the many elements of explanations, Robert Guest writes that 'Africans often do not trust each other' and he continues to comment 'I have seen plenty of evidence that lack of trust makes it harder to get things done in Africa' (2005: 193). This may be relevant in our context since one partial explanation that social scientists come up with for Norway's present fortune is that Norwegians have a tendency to trust each other and the political institutions in the country (Repstad 2005). Daniel Branch (2011) points in the same direction in his book *Kenya. Between hope and despair, 1963 – 2011.* He mentions ethnically based networks through which information and opportunities may be distributed. The reciprocal ties between members within the same ethnic group allows for extension of credit and more confidence in the goods and services bought from someone with common ethnic identity. It is all founded on trust.

Trust – a great asset

Trust promotes seamless interaction

This trust makes social interaction more seamless and less costly. When you trust that the other will not cheat you, deceive you or lie to you, you save time, energy and money and build relationships that lift you up. Trust therefore

43

seems to be a good recipe for prosperity. In a society where people trust each other reciprocity is very likely to happen and human dignity is strengthened.

Trust may be challen-ged

I was working on this chapter in July 2011 just as a twofold action of terror took place in Norway, the worst in this part of Europe since World War II. The first was a bomb blast against cabinet and other government offices in the central part of the capital city Oslo. The second was the shooting of many young people at a summer camp for the Norwegian labour party, about an hour's drive from the capital. This peaceful country was all of a sudden faced with the challenge that one of her own young men had taken advantage of and violated the culture of trust and killed 77 people and seriously wounded a similar number, in addition to leaving parts of downtown Oslo resembling a war zone. The immediate reaction was shock and disbelief, but also that of persistence: this evil deed shall not be allowed to erode our trust and compassion for each other. The long-term consequences are yet to be seen. Will the Norwegian society become less trusting and less open, with less solidarity and love? Or will the Norwegian people manage to stand up for their culture and turn this terrible event into an asset? Through trials and tribulations a people may become more aware of their culture's strong points and become even more motivated to preserve and further develop such points. Hopefully this will be the case for the Norwegian citizens after this cruel act.

2.2.3 Reconciliation

To live truthfully

Sometimes we succeed. We are able to accomplish what we want and set out to do. It is wonderful when this happens. But sometimes we do not succeed. So, when we do wrong and fail the 'cause', our fellow men, our family, our own ideals etc., we may put our failures aside, we may forget them or pretend to forget them. There are many strategies of avoidance. Nevertheless, to live with dignity means to live truthfully. In order to handle failure well, we need to face it and that may be done in three steps. For the perpetrator that means 1) to admit wrongdoing, 2) to ask forgiveness and 3) to do what may be possible to compensate for any loss that is a consequence of the wrongdoing. For the suffering party it means first to recognize the offender's concession and request for pardon, second to appraise and third to act on the questions of forgiveness and compensation. To be held accountable for one's words and acts is actually a deed of human dignity for the offending as well as the suffering party. The main challenge in addition to the psychological endurance is to strike a balance between the three steps described above. These three steps of reconciliation apply to individual and social level both.

Failure should be faced

Reconciliation implies to give away something. For the perpetrator it may mean to give away pride and any possible gain from the offence. For the offended, it may mean to give away the 'right' to revenge and hatred. Here it could be pointed at the numerous processes of peace and reconciliation that have been made on the African continent after insane violence towards civil populations that have stunned the world. In his book, *Africa Altered states, ordinary miracles*, Richard Dowden writes: 'Given some of the atrocities that have occurred in Africa's wars, I am always struck by the spirit of forgiveness when they end. [...] Africa seems to have a talent for reconciliation when wars finally end.' (2009: 305). Here is an important point where Africa may be a significant inspiration to the rest of the world, providing that this talent for reconciliation includes the ability not only to forgive, but also to learn – lest the atrocities may reappear.

A talent for reconcil- iation

2.2.4 Material goods[7]

To harvest from own work

From what is written above, it should be clear that human dignity does not depend on what human beings possess of material goods, but is grounded on the mere fact of being human. Human dignity is recognised for instance in the exercise of self-expression, self-determination, self-affirmation and by working and being allowed to harvest the benefits from one's work. Therefore, it should be obvious that when others deny a person access to material benefits from her/his own resources, natural resources included, the effect of this is that the dignity of this person is eroded. Such dynamics are similar on aggregate as well as individual level and this was strongly exemplified during colonialism. Through the exploitation of African natural resources, African peoples were robbed not only of their natural resources, but also of their value as human beings. The slave trade had even stronger consequences in this respect. Unfortunately, it may be noted that after the colonial period, a substantial part of African leadership has been stained by corruption, dictatorial tendencies, patron – client-relationships and mismanagement of both physical and human resources. This kind of leadership has prolonged the lowering of the dignity of African peoples lasting up to this day. And it is observed that material poverty evolves into a poverty of the mind, killing human dignity and the self-worth of the people (Lumumba 2008).

Material poverty evolves into poverty of the mind

This observation leads to the conclusion that there is a connection between poverty and the erosion of human dignity, even if we insist (as we should) that human dignity does not rest on material goods.

2.3 The triangle of human dignity and ways to strengthen it

As we further develop our understanding of the concept of human dignity, it becomes obvious that this understanding

---

[7] This part draws heavily on Rutto & Njoroge 2001 for content and wording.

must be turned into action and have consequences in our daily lives – on personal as well as community level. Here is a set of self-enforcing dynamics in action: the more we understand, the more we see the need to act. And the more we act, the better we understand the concept. The effect of this is that human dignity is strengthened. It is like training a muscle by flexing it.

Understanding and acting are intertwined

In his book *Social reconstruction of Africa*, Stein Villumstad (2005) offers some interesting ideas in this context. He suggests that human dignity may be especially strengthened through putting the three concepts of Human Rights, Human Development and Human Security into action, as illustrated in a triangle of human dignity, figure 2.

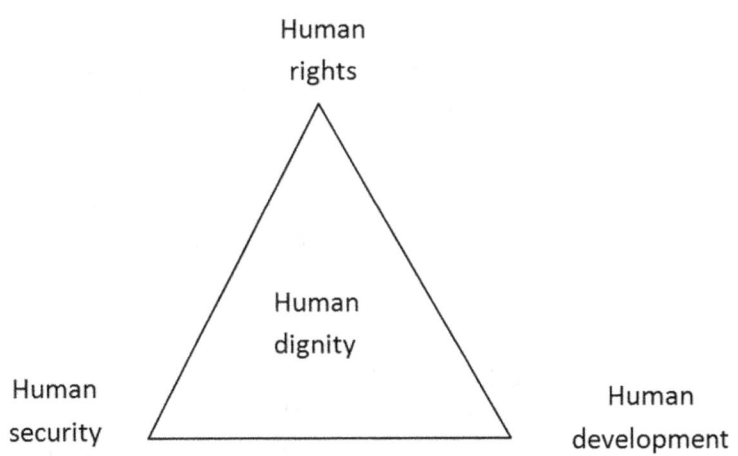

Figure 2: The triangle of human dignity (Villumstad 2005).

2.3.1 Human rights

Human rights is about access to food, basic health and education, religious freedom, no discrimination based on race, colour, gender, language, religion, political or other opinion, national or social origin, property, birth or other status. The Universal Declaration on Human Rights (DHR)[8] is quite specific on what is regarded as the rights that any human being has per se. Villumstad points out that fulfilment of human rights are focused on the present generation, but the challenges of degradation which shows as pollution, climate change, loss of biodiversity, mismanagement of land and water pose a variety of threats to sustainability of living conditions in the future.

DHR is focused on the present generation

The DHR has a lot of concrete statements on what is right and what is wrong, for example:

Article 3: Everyone has the right to life, liberty and security of person.

Article 4: No one shall be held in slavery or servitude; slavery and the slave trade shall be prohibited in all their forms.

Article 5: No one shall be subjected to torture or to cruel, inhuman or degrading treatment or punishment.

DHR: How to act for the good

There are 30 articles. These statements are advising us how to act for the good anywhere in the world. We, as individuals as well as societies, certainly need that help. Human rights have the very important advantage that they may be enforced. It is relatively easy to know when human rights are being violated. Perpetrators may be brought to book by agents of law-enforcement. That has a disciplining effect and strengthens security for people in general. As we look closely, we see that these articles actually advise us how to act in accordance with human dignity.

---

[8] See The Universal Declaration on Human Rights:
http://www.un.org/en/documents/udhr/

2.3.2 Human development

Human development is a process where the living conditions of people are improved. This improvement include moral growth (i.e. honesty, trustworthiness, willingness to suffer for the greater cause), growth of social skills (i.e. humility, respect, empathy, inclination for dialogue, self-fulfilment) and mental growth (i.e. cognitive skills, objectivity, open-mindedness, tolerance). Rutto & Njoroge emphasize these human aspects as they describe development as 'a search for the good, the true and the just while realizing oneself to greater heights of personal fulfilment and dignity' (2001: 53).

Human development includes moral and mental growth

For many practical purposes, human development should also be presented statistically. For a long time the measurements of human welfare and development were mainly economic indicators like Gross National Income per inhabitant. Although useful in many ways, this proved to be not only insufficient, but could also be a threat to the *human* aspects of development for societies. The UN therefore worked out the Human Development Index (HDI), where Life expectancy at birth, Education and Gross National Income per capita are assessed. This index was presented in 1990 (UN 1990) and was a substantial step forward in the ambition to come beyond the dominance of economic concerns in the measurement of human welfare and development. Since 1990 continuous work has been done for further improvement among which some of the most important have been to include distribution of factors of well-being, empowerment and sustainability. The HDI is based on statistical average of life expectancy, education and income and we know that neither of these are evenly distributed in a population. Therefore efforts are made to include distribution in order to check inequality between genders, social groups, geographical regions etc. In the Human Development Report 2010 and 2011 this is done in table 3 headlined 'Inequality-adjusted Human Development Index' (IHDI). Another important betterment is a focus on people's ability to influence decisions that are taken on behalf of society as

HDI presents statistics on human development: life expectancy, education and income

Distribution, empowerment and sustainability should be added

a whole, in one word: empowerment and the UN emphasise the importance of this as mentioned above. The third field is about environmental degradation. Here the need for improvements has become ever more pressing especially with sustainability and the direction of future development in mind.

Building on the Human Development Report 1990 and later works, Human development may be summed up as being about increasing people's abilities and possibilities to choose, - today and in the time to come.

2.3.3. Human security

Human security is about including the human dimension into general discussions of security. The idea is to place human beings at the focal point of security considerations rather than the states. 'Freedom from fear' has become a catch phrase for this approach (UNDIR 2011).

Peace and stability on all levels

'Human security is about peace and stability on all levels' (Villumstad 2005: 16). Violence in all its appearances undermine human security: domestic violence, gender based violence, age based violence, violence based on ethnicity, threats and actions of terror in peaceful societies, violence in war against civilians as well as troops. Brutality within these and other fields and of all kinds restrict possibilities for free movement and tend to paralyze production within all sectors and activities, be it agriculture, pastoralism, industry, service, education, health, religion, science or other. This is the case whether the production is for self-sufficiency or for the market. It is taking place within the formal or informal sector, and is of political as well as civil kind. It also does not distinguish between geographical levels; home, village, district, nation, region or global. In short: it affects all sorts of human life

Affects all and everything

individually as well as socially. The many and different threats of insecurity deteriorate all aspects of human life and inflict physical and psychological trauma on people involved. When the threats are realised in actions of violence, as too often is the case, this expands and aggravates the devastating consequences (Villumstad 2005).

A brief search on the internet shows that for the time being, controlling small arms, land mines, hunger, disease, environmental contamination and disasters are taken to be central challenges in the efforts to promote human security. Not to forget the need to secure industrial and service production sites, neighbourhoods and public grounds.

2.3.4 Interaction between the three

There are of course dynamics between the three and they are in many ways intertwined and influence each other. Villumstad (2005: 17-18) explains that

- Human Rights contribute to human development and human security through promoting good governance, social justice and rule of law.
- Human security facilitates human development and supports human rights through providing peace and stability.
- Human development enhances both human rights and human security through addressing social and economic perspectives.

As the three corners in this triangle (figure 2) are addressed, human dignity is promoted.

2.4 Human dignity – a question of the heart

While human rights, human security and human development are essential ways to materialize human dignity, it is important to realize that human dignity is of a different and higher order than the others. Since I find this most clear in the relationship between human rights and human dignity, I will use this as my example in an effort to explain.

Enforce-able and unenforce-able obligations

The Declaration of Human Rights (DHR) with its 30 articles states quite clearly what is right and what is wrong. As mentioned above, these rules are specific enough that they may be followed up by law-enforcement agencies, be it on local, national or international level. In his speech 'On being a good neighbour', Martin Luther King jr. gives credit to Dr. Harry Emerson Fosdick for making a clear distinction between enforceable and unenforceable obligations. While written laws and regulations like DHR may be enforced and punishment distributed to those who violate against them, 'unenforceable obligations are beyond the reach of the laws of society' (1982: 33). King continues to explain: 'They [the unenforceable obligations] concern inner attitudes, genuine person to person relations and expressions of compassion which law books cannot regulate and jails cannot rectify. Such obligations are met by one's commitment to an inner law, written on the heart. Man-made laws assure justice, but a higher law produces love'. There are so many situations in life that are not, and cannot be covered by laws and regulations. These are situations where concepts like encouragement, help, compassion and love better describe the needed or wanted response than paragraphs in any written law. What can be enforced is very much about the surface of things, of how a person behaves. What may not be enforced is much about inner properties, about the person's values and attitudes. There may be a parallel in what money can buy and what it cannot buy, as described by the Norwegian author Arne Garborg: money can buy company but not friendship, medicine but not health, fun but not joy, food but not appetite, soft beds but not sleep etc. Money can

A distinct-ion between rules and fair play

buy material necessities but the inner satisfaction is of a higher order and cannot be bought for money. Another example may be the relationship between rules and fair play in sports like football. King describes this as the habits and the heart:

'Morality cannot be legislated, but behaviour can be regulated. Judicial decrees may not change the heart, but they can restrain the heartless. [...] The habits, if not the hearts, of people have been and are being altered every day by legislative acts, judicial decisions and executive orders' (1982: 34). So there should be no reason to belittle the effects of Human Rights. Nonetheless, the motivation and energy to surpass written rules lies in the attitudes, in the set of personal, committing values. And that is what makes life not only secure, but in essence real human. That is what the nature of human dignity is about. The person who has this attitude in the heart does not stop at observing the rights of a human being in the way the DHR presents them. This person also responds to the obligations and responsibilities that must be put into action to create a desirable society, even if inactivity in such matters cannot and will not be punished legally. From all this it may be derived that to have responsibilities and obligations is something that gives us dignity. We have an active role to play in society.

Habits and the heart

I find backing for the idea that the heart is utmost important in something Julius Nyerere is reported to have said. Nyerere is recognised to be the 'father' of the nation Tanzania. As a distinguished freedom fighter and the country's first president (1962 – 1985) he was responsible for planning and implementing a number of political actions with the aim to improve the living conditions of the citizens. Some of these policies were partly realised by the use of force.

The heart and development

Attitudes surpass written rules

Towards the end of his life, Nyerere told Bishop Bartolomayo Jonathan that he had come to the conclusion that nothing will change in society unless the hearts of people change[9].

Human behavior is regulated from the outside and the inside

To sum up: Individual human behaviour may be regulated in two ways: from the outside and from the inside. Enforceable laws and regulations represent the outside. The unenforceable, internalized values, attitudes and obligations, represent the inside. As individuals and as a society we need both. Kobia claims: 'All human rights flow from the recognition and affirmation of the dignity of the individual person' (2003, referred in Villumstad 2005: 14). This actually means that the outer ways of regulating human behaviour are derived from, builds on the inner ways. As shown above, there are good reasons to support this view. Along with such support, an addition should be made: human dignity surpasses human rights into action on unenforceable obligations and responsibilities in an attitude of compassion and love. Love is trustworthy, durable and creative and supports the notion that human dignity is of a higher order.

2.5 Human dignity and democracy

Many strong links between human dignity and democracy

A fundamental presumption in this chapter is that the concept of human dignity connects with democracy where the former is an important value base for the latter. The former Norwegian prime minister, Kjell Magne Bondevik states in a newspaper article that democracy is a natural consequence of human dignity (Vårt Land 16.01.13). Based on quiet studies of his domestic animals (pigs and calves) a Zimbabwean farmer claimed that 'nature knows nothing

---

[9] Julius Nyerere had his home in the village Butiama in Mara district close to Lake Victoria. At a convention for clergymen in Mara Diocese in 1992, bishop Bartolomayo Jonathan related this information that surfaced during a conversation he relatively recently had had with Nyerere.

about democracy' (Lessing 1993: 227). I think that he is right. Democracy is about *human* beings taking charge, founded on human dignity. Human dignity is the fundamental value, the leading star that should inspire our actions on all levels, individually and socially. This has a lot of implications where the individual, societies like NGOs and government bodies as well as villages, need to be considerate and creative in finding ways and actions that are based on and strengthen human dignity. Democratic thought, principles and procedures have many characteristics that support this: respect for individual and social freedom, rule of law, transparency, accountability and opportunity to participate. The links between human dignity and democracy are many and strong. Many and strong in such ways that the title of this chapter should be appropriate: Human Dignity [is] the Core Value of Democracy. Consequently, an efficient way to strengthen democracy is to strengthen human dignity in its many aspects.

Study questions for Chapter 2

1. Give reasons why humans deserve a special kind of dignity compared with other beings.
2. What is respect about and why is respect an important aspect of human dignity?
3. What is reciprocity about and why is reciprocity an important aspect of human dignity?
4. What is reconciliation about and why is reconciliation an important aspect of human dignity?
5. This chapter claims that respect, reciprocity and reconciliation are three important aspects of human dignity. Add some more aspects to the list and explain why you think they deserve to be on your list.
6. How can we recognize human dignity in our everyday life?
7. Describe what is meant by human rights.
8. Describe what is meant by human development.
9. Describe what is meant by human security.
10. Describe and explain the 'Triangle of human dignity' and by so doing, explain how human dignity is strengthened through the exercise of human rights, human development and human security.
11. Explain why human dignity is of a higher order than human rights and what consequences this should have in our lives.
12. Explain how human dignity and democracy are connected.

References

Dowden, R (2009): *Africa. Altered states, ordinary miracles* London: Portobello Books Ltd.

Dysthe, O (1999): 'Læring gjennom dialog – kva inneber det i høgare utdanning?' In Dysthe, O (red) *Ulike perspektiv på læring og læringsforskning* Oslo: Cappelen Akademisk Forlag.

Fløistad, G (1996): *Om å kunne mer enn man kan. Verdiformidling, kunnskapskrav og ledelse i skolen* Kristiansand: HøyskoleForlaget.

King, M. L jr. (1982): *Strength to love* Glasgow: William Collins Sons & Co Ltd.

Kobia, S (2003): *The Courage to Hope. A Challenge for Churches in Africa* Nairobi: Acton Publishers.

Lessing, D (1993): *African Laughter. Four visits to Zimbabwe* London: Flamingo.

Lumumba, P. L. O (2008): *A call for Hygiene in Kenyan Politics.* Nairobi: MvuleAfrica Publishers.

Maathai, W (2009): *The Challenge for Africa. A New Vision.* London: William Heineman Random House.

Phillips, D. T (1998): *Martin Luther King jr. On Leadership. Inspiration & wisdom for challenging times.* New York: Warner Books.

Repstad, P (2005): 'Norway – An Egalitarian Society?' In Magerø, E & B Simonsen: *Norway: Society and Culture.* Kristiansand: Portal.

Rutto, S. K and G. K Njoroge (2001): *The democratization process in Africa* Nairobi: Quest & Insight.

Solhaug, T and K. Børhaug (2012): *Skolen i demokratiet. Demokratiet i skolen.* Oslo: Universitetsforlaget.

UN (1990): *Human Development report 1990. Concept and Measurement of human development* http://hdr.undp.org/en/reports/global/hdr1990/chapters/

UN (2002): *Human Development Report 2002. Deepening Democracy in a Fragmented World* http://hdr.undp.org/en/reports/global/hdr2002/

UN (2004): *Human Development Report 2004. Cultural Liberty in Today's Diverse World* http://hdr.undp.org/en/reports/global/hdr2004/

UN (2005): *Human Development Report. International cooperation at a crossroads: Aid, trade and security in an unequal world* http://hdr.undp.org/en/reports/global/hdr2005/

UN (2006): *Human Development Report 2006. Beyond scarcity: Power, poverty and the global water crisis* http://hdr.undp.org/en/reports/global/hdr2006/

UN (2007/2008): *Human Development Report 2007/2008. Fighting climate change: Human solidarity in a divided world* http://hdr.undp.org/en/reports/global/hdr2007-2008/

UN (2009): *Human Development Report 2009. Overcoming barriers: Human mobility and development* http://hdr.undp.org/en/reports/global/hdr2009/

UN (2010): *Human Development Report 2010. 20th Anniversary Edition. The Real Wealth of Nations: Pathways to Human Development* http://hdr.undp.org/en/reports/global/hdr2010/chapters/

UN (2011): Human Development Report 2011. *Sustainability and Equity: A Better Future for All* http://hdr.undp.org/en/media/HDR_2011_EN_Complete.pdf

UNDIR (United Nations Institute for Disarmament Research) (2011): Human security http://www.unidir.org/html/en/human_security.html.

Villumstad, S (2005): *Social Reconstruction of Africa. Perspectives from Within and Without* Nairobi: Acton Publishers.

Washington, J. M (ed.) (1991): *A testament of hope. The Essential Writings and Speeches of Martin Luther King, Jr.* New York: HarperCollinsPublisher.

Chapter 3

IS DEMOCRACY *(ONLY)* A WESTERN CONCEPT?

"Democratic principles and attitudes transcend subjective limitations. Admittedly, they may be manifested variably in different cultures and circumstances but the vision and the spirit within which they are practised is identically expressed across cultures. The argument that democracy is a purely subjective idea or affair is, therefore, not tenable" — Rutto & Njoroge

3.1 Are there links to democracy in African culture?

From time to time it is claimed that democracy mainly is a Western concept and that the introduction of democracy to Africa therefore is a version of updated colonialism which in addition promotes capitalism. Mobuto Sese Seko may be taken to support this view as he claimed that 'democracy is not for Africa' (Guest 2005: 46). This was while he was the president of Zaire, today's Democratic Republic of Congo. He certainly proved that it was possible to be head of an African country and run a government with few, if any, characteristics of democracy. There are a number of more or less similar examples. Aseka (1996) mentions for instance that the building of democratic structures in Africa has not been very successful. Claude Ake (2003) writes that '…in too many countries in Africa, democratization is little more than an

Unsuccessful democratic structures

opening for elites who were previously excluded from power [during colonization] to compete for it' (2003: 73). Even so, he also claims that 'Africa has come a long way with democratization but there is still a very long way to go.' (ibid: 74). Be that as it may, the aim here is not to point out the obvious: that there are many African societies where democratic ways and means are given little respect. On the contrary, the aim of this chapter is to give examples and reasons for the conviction that there are many features in African history, culture and present societies which support the view that democracy is not foreign to the African continent. This should be something similar to what is claimed for Asia (Smith 2007). Wangari Maathai wrote that 'the lack of self-knowledge that comes from Africans' cultural deracination is one of the most troubling and long-lasting effects of colonialism' (2009: 34). She continued to argue that this lack of self-knowledge has contributed to the growth of a culture of dependency where the people's own capacity and responsibility to act is increasingly weakened. As a consequence many Africans expect initiatives and actions for improvements to come from outside. Therefore it is an ambition for this chapter to contribute to some Africa knowledge. If the idea that democracy also has roots in African culture is accepted, this may be beneficial at least in two ways. Firstly, it may strengthen the motivation for Africans to further develop democracy as a good system of governance in their context. There is no doubt that there is ample room for improved governance in many African societies. Here societies of different kinds and different levels are relevant: national, regional and local government; different institutions within education, health care, religion, business and nongovernmental organizations (NGOs). It may also include the private sphere like family life. Secondly, African heritage and experience may offer important contributions to a continuous development of democracy, not only in Africa, but around the globe.

A lack of self knowledge

Room for improve- ment in govern- ment

Africa may contribute to democratic development

3.2 Characteristics different from democratic ideals

In his paper 'The Democratic myth in the African

Traditional Societies' the historian Simiyu claims that in African history there is no clear cut democratic tradition, but rather 'various mixtures of rudimentary democratic institutions and despotism' (1987: 51). On the not-so democratic side he characterizes African societies in general as hierarchical, with social structures where upward mobility is very much restricted and an age-set system that favours the older age-groups. Rutto & Njoroge support and expand this view as they claim that '…the young and women are often given a peripheral role in decision making. Even when these groups are given a hearing, their suggestions are usually not taken seriously' (2001: 62). These are societies where the rights of the individual usually are subordinate to the needs of the community, for instance in questions of peace and social equilibrium. Take the example that an individual has been violated against and the question of compensation is on the agenda. According to African tradition the main focus will be on finding a solution where life can safely go on for the relevant social group that the victim belongs to, be it family, clan, village or any other. A solution where individual justice be done and individual compensation be given to the victim, will have a lower priority. Simiyu claims that the characteristics mentioned above are very much different from the democratic ideals of individual human rights, self- determination and the right for citizens to decide how they shall be ruled and who shall rule them. It may however be mentioned that also in well developed democracies the needs of the fellowship may often overrule the needs, or even the rights of the individual (see for instance Smith 2007). Individual interests and needs must be harmonised with social interests and needs. The question of resource allocation may illustrate this. In any society, a democracy included, a patient may not get the treatment s/he needs because the fellowship spends the available resources for other purposes. This may happen even though the individual right to such treatment may be written into the law. Nonetheless, I find Simiyu's argument plausible that a democracy generally will honour individual rights stronger than the African societies he describes.

The fellowship is given priority over the individual person

3.3 Some African examples of democratic ways and means

Rudiments of democratic principles and practices

Among a few examples of rudiments of democratic features Simiyu mentions that the sense of equality among age-mates is very strong and that the army sometimes offers a possible road for upward social mobility. Even so, he maintains that 'In Black Africa, whether the political system was that of the highly centralized states or of the amorphous non-centralized communities, it did not belong to a democratic tradition. There were rudiments of democratic principles and practices, especially in the non-centralized communities, but it would be dangerous to equate those practices with advanced forms of democracy' (ibid: 68).

3.3.1 Government by discussion

Nyerere: traditional African democracy

The late Tanzanian statesman, Julius Nyerere, on the other hand, seems to find more than rudiments of democracy in African culture. He even claimed that there is such a thing as a 'traditional African democracy' of which discussion, equality and freedom are essential characteristics (Kweka 1995:65). He emphasizes the tradition of free discussions and the principles of consensus as typical African examples of 'government by discussion' (Green 1995, Simiyu 1995) and is cited to have said in this connection: '...convince, but do not force, argue, but do not shout' (Othman, referred in Mmari 1995: 181).

3.3.2 Ujima

Wamwere: pre-colonial African egalitarianism

In the newspaper Daily Nation of Nairobi (22.06.11) the Kenyan politician Koigi wa Wamwere presents the concept of 'ujima' which he describes as pre-colonial African egalitarianism: '*Ujima* was a system of humanism, harmony and generational democracy that brooked no dictatorship and put public welfare before individual interests and greed. Under egalitarianism, there was no money- or devil-worship. A good name was everything. Everybody had a right to food. Nothing excused theft. Courage defined character. Children were cared for and corrected by all. Everyone was his brother's keeper. Wisdom, not wealth, determined leadership.' Wamwere then describes how this egalitarianism through time embraced more individual greed and thus paved the way for capitalism and colonial values, which he does not find especially democratic.

3.3.3 Village meeting

The Ghanaian scholar George Ayittey points in a similar direction as he also explains from the pre-colonial tradition: 'When crises erupted in an African village, the chief and the elders would summon a village meeting. There, the issue was debated by the people until a consensus was reached. During the debate, the chief usually made no effort to manipulate the outcome or sway public opinion. Nor were there bazooka-wielding rouges intimidating or instructing people on what they should say. People expressed their ideas openly and freely without fear of arrest' (Guest 2005: 71-72).

In time of crisis people discussed freely in search for a solution

3.3.4 Make up and speak one's mind

Another example is presented by the Nigerian writer Chinua Achebe as he describes the tradition where the Igbo search for the balance between the needs of the individual and the needs of the community. They would organize 'a popular assembly that is small enough for everybody who wishes to be present to do so and to "speak his own mouth" as they like to phrase it' (Achebe 2001: 15). Considering the combination of this institution, the general struggle for life and a disinclination to accept a ruler like a king, it should surprise nobody that the British, according to Achebe, characterized the Igbo in general as argumentative. To survive he had better make up his mind and speak it, a fundamental quality for any democrat.

The Igbo was described as argumenta-tive by the British

3.3.5 Harambee

An act of neighbourly responsibility

In Kenyan context 'harambee' is an important feature in political as well as social life. Harambee means 'pulling together' or putting our hands together for a special cause or some common good. It may be about constructing a school or water pipe, it may be someone needing help to pay for a funeral, a hospital bill or something else of importance. So 'everybody' chips in, as an act of fellowship, neighbourly love, solidarity or in short taking responsibility for each other. It seems plausible to associate harambee with a democratic mindset.

3.3.6 Ujamaa

Relocation to make amenities more commonly available

Sharing of decision making is clearly a democratic feature

The policy of 'ujamaa' on Tanzanian turf was founded on an idea similar to harambee. Ujamaa means 'family-hood and mutual involvement of all family members for the fellowship' (Komba 1995: 37). During the 1970s rural people in Tanzania were assembled in special ujamaa villages. Here the inhabitants were supposed to share duties and jobs in such an organized manner that a larger variety of services than before could be available and the infrastructure like good roads, clean water, health services and education could be more easily available to more people. Since the majority of the Tanzanians were rural peasants, an important part of the ujamaa policy focused on improving agricultural practices. This was easier to achieve if people lived in villages rather than scattered in the countryside. Today rather few seem to regard the ujamaa policy as successful, but that may be just as much because of the way it was implemented than the idea itself. The sharing of responsibilities in villages, including decision making, is clearly linked to democratic ways. And there is no doubt that president Nyerere regarded the ujamaa philosophy as something genuine African as he stressed the need to 'build upon the foundation of our past, and building also to our design' (ibid: 37).

3.3.7 Proverbs and storytelling

Moto (1998) and Chidam'modzi (1999) present a lot of examples of features in Malawian traditional systems of governance, proverbs and storytelling that easily may be associated with democracy: social responsibility, discipline, conversation and dialogue, freedom of expression, the need to tolerate and respect other people's opinions and choices, the need for accountability and transparency, an impartial, just and independent judicial system and the rule of law. Moto claims that 'proverbs and folk stories provide overwhelming evidence that democracy as a concept is not a totally new way of viewing how communities should be governed, but rather that democratic practice, ideals and principles are deeply embedded in the fabric of Malawian society' (1998: 24).

Overwhelming evidence that democracy is deeply embedded in Malawian society

3.3.8 A second liberation

The political scientist Claude Ake endorses democracy in a classic sense and characterizes this as 'the realization of human potentialities through active participation in rulership' (1996: 14). He is convinced that this democracy is not given from the persons or groups who presently are in power. The people has to take it – most probably through the use of some power. While the first struggle for independence was against the colonizing powers, the second, and present one is against their own, post-colonial political leaders. A certain detachment from the latter may be instrumental to obtain it. In this context he points to the associational life in rural Africa of which he offers a number of examples, i.e. craft centres, rural credit unions, farmers' associations, community-run skill development centres, community-financed schools and hospitals and civic centres. He indicates that such associations may be people's response to a state that does not deliver the services and actions for development that they need or want. So they may retreat from the state to the community or primary group as they try 'to possess their own development' (ibid: 46), realizing their human potentialities.

3.3.9 Inputs from a workshop

At a workshop for DAFI students[10] in June 2011, in essence the content above in this chapter was presented. In essence the content above in this chapter was presented. In addition the relationship between democracy and human dignity was strongly underlined. There is a reciprocity between the two: democracy is built on human dignity and human dignity is strengthened through democratic ways and means[11]. After this teaching participants were asked to look for traces of democracy in their African culture(s) (since they were all African refugees they could identify with more than one culture) that they regarded themselves to be part of. This was organised as a combination of individual and group work and a number of points were made.

During the discussion several statements were made on organizing in the village, where different aspects of rule of law, which is fundamental in democracy, in one way or the other were mentioned: 'There are rules set to be followed in the community' and people have 'Respect for society customs, laws and regulations'. One of the rules that was mentioned is that 'Your family is held accountable if you commit a crime and run'. The chief's role is pivotal: For one, it is claimed that the chief is elected and carries out fair judgment. Even so, 'Community leaders have meetings with the chief to discuss issues in the community' and the chief may also take the initiative for consultations: 'When a problem arises in the community, the chief informs the people to hear their views to find an appropriate solution'. In line with this goes the claim from one participant that there is 'freedom of expression in politics' in this person's village. One participant mentioned that the fellowship is intentionally built: 'There are celebrations that unite people'. This unity inspires actions: 'Funeral contributions are almost mandatory'; 'Carrying the sick to the health

There are celebra-tions that unite people

---

[10] http://dafischolars.org/index.php/dafi/history/item/60-1992-1995
[11] See the chapter 2 for more details on this subject

centre is the responsibility of every male member above 18'
and 'There is also community work organized to help
disadvantaged ones'. In these statements neighbourly love
and solidarity based on respect for human dignity shine
through. Transparency is an important trait of democracy
and the following statement may indicate something in that
direction: 'Everybody has the right to ask for identification
from any person new in the community'. Only a few
statements focus on the family level and the two following
point in different directions: 'At home family members sit
down to discuss issues and share problems' and 'In the
home the father rules'. It may be suggested that the latter
example probably is more common in African homes than
the former. Nonetheless, the former indicates that African
homes should be(-come) an important arena for fostering
democracy.

Trans-
parency

3.4 Democracy focuses on the people and is part of their culture

In a nutshell democracy is described as governance of, by
and for the people[12]. *Of the people* indicates that the
governance is in accordance with the peoples' way of life,
the culture of the society. *By the people* means that people
influence decisions made on behalf of the society through
their participation. *For the people* implies that the
government's decisions should benefit the members of the
community in a number of ways (Githonga, 1987). From
this it is obvious that depending on culture, history and
situation, the brand of democracy should be expected to
differ between countries. Even so, the value of human
dignity with its many and far reaching implications should
be taken as universal and should not be compromised as
the ideal of democracy: Human dignity is the core value of
democracy, and human dignity is in no way an exclusive
Western phenomenon.

Human
dignity – the
core value

---

[12] US president Abraham Lincoln in a famous speech of 1863, called the Gettysburg
Address, described representative democracy as 'government of the people, by the people
and for the people.'

In our days Western countries may dominate the rhetoric and generally do well on measures of democratic governance. Augustine Titani Magolowondo (2013) suggests that much is just about choice of words as he discusses civic education in Malawi: 'People in the villages appreciate the importance of communities and good neighborliness. They appreciate the role the leaders play and are able to question them when they conduct not according to the expectation of society. It is only when terms such as democracy and human rights are presented to them often in a foreign language and by people who seem to be foreigners too that suddenly, everything becomes "new".' So the Western countries have no exclusive right neither to the principles, practices nor rhetoric of democracy.

Democracy should be connected to the indigenous culture

Therefore every country, be it African, Asian, Western or other, must develop her own democracy. The challenge is to connect with own culture and history and blend it with the values, ideas, attitudes and practices supportive of human dignity. When approaching the challenge in these ways, democracy may be (re)captured as a feasible system for governance at any geographical, social or political level be it in Africa or anywhere else.

1. In what ways may it be beneficial to establish whether democracy also has roots in African culture?
2. In general the needs of the community override the needs and rights of the individual. In this chapter it is claimed that this is more often the case in traditional African cultures compared to developed democracies. Is this description in accordance with your experience / impression?
3. How did Nyerere describe what he called 'traditional African democracy'?
4. Explain in what ways the concept of 'ujima' contains democratic features.
5. Name different African examples where decisions are reached through general discussion.
6. In this chapter we read: 'It seems plausible to associate harambee with a democratic mind-set'. Do you agree or disagree? Explain your view.
7. In what ways was the policy of ujamaa villages in Tanzania democratic? Do you find undemocratic features in this policy?
8. From your own culture, can you give any example(s) of stories and/or proverbs that may be linked to democracy? If so, write down the story/stories and proverb(s) and explain how you connect it with democracy.
9. Give an example of a trace of democracy from your own culture and explain in what way(s) you find this democratic.
10. Why may different societies be differently democratic and what is the all important feature of democracy in any society?
11. This chapter concludes that democracy is not only a Western concept, but a universal one. Do you agree or disagree? Explain your view / conclusion.

References

Achebe, C (2001): *Home and Exile* New York: Anchor Books.

Ake, C (2003): *The Feasibility of Democracy in Africa.* Oxford: African Books Collective.

Aseka, E. M (1996): *Africa in the 21st Century* Eldoret: Zapf Chancery Research Consultants & Publishers.

Chidam'modzi, H.F (1999): 'Democracy and tradition in Malawi'. In Chimombo, M. *Lessons in Hope: Education for Democracy in Malawi, Past, Present, Future.* Zomba: National Chancellor College Publications.

Githonga, A.K. (1995): 'The meaning and foundations of democracy.' In Oyugi, W.O and A.K Githonga (eds.), *Democratic theory and practice in Africa.* Nairobi: East African Education Publishers.

Green, R. H (1995): 'Vision of Human-Centered Development: A Study in Moral Economy'. In Legum, C and G Mmari: *Mwalimu. The Influence of Nyerere.* London / Dar es Salaam / Trenton: James Currey / Mkuki na Nyota / Africa World Press.

Guest, R (2005): *The Shackled Continent. Africa's Past, Present and Future.* London: Pan Books.

Komba, D (1995): 'Contribution to Rural Development: Ujamaa & Villagisation'. In Legum, C and G. Mmari: *Mwalimu. The Influence of Nyerere.* London / Dar es Salaam / Trenton: James Currey / Mkuki na Nyota / Africa World Press.

Kweka, A. N (1995): 'One-Party Democracy & the Multi-Party State'. In Legum, C and G. Mmari: *Mwalimu. The Influence of Nyerere.* London / Dar es Salaam / Trenton: James Currey / Mkuki na Nyota / Africa World Press.

Maathai, W (2009): *The Challenge for Africa. A New Vision.* London: William Heineman Random House.

Magolowondo, A. T (2013): 'Critical Challenges Facing Civic Education Provision in Malawi'. *In Non partisan magazine THE LAMP Christians, Politics & Culture.* Balaka: Montfort Media.

Mmari, G (1995): 'The Legacy of Nyerere' In Legum, C and G Mmari: *Mwalimu. The Influence of Nyerere.* London / Dar es Salaam / Trenton: James Currey / Mkuki na Nyota / Africa World Press.

Moto, F (1998): 'Domesticating the Definition of Democracy'. In Tsoka, M and C. Mikey, *Bwalo. A forum for social development*, Issue 2. Zomba: University of Malawi.

Rutto, S. K and G. K Njoroge (2001): *The democratization process in Africa* Nairobi: Quest & Insight.

Simiyu, V.G (1995): 'The Democratic Myth in the African Traditional Societies.' In Oyugi, W.O and A.K Githonga (eds.), *Democratic theory and practice in Africa.* Nairobi: East African Education Publishers.

Smith, B. C (2007): *Good Governance and Development* Hampshire / New York: Palgrave MacMillan.

Wamwere, K (2011): 'It's capitalism that has mothered our moral decadence as a society.' In Daily Nation June 22nd 2011. Nairobi.

PART TWO

LEADERSHIP

Chapter 4

UNDERSTANDING LEADERSHIP

At the 1991 IAAF World Athletics Championships in Osaka, Japan, the US team assembled Andrew Valmon, Quincy Watts (who would go on to break the 400m Olympic record twice at the 1992 Olympic Games in Barcelona, Spain), Danny Everett (the bronze medallist in the 400m at the Games) and Antonio Pettigrew (the 400m world champion) to run the first, second, third and fourth legs respectively in the 4 by 400m final race. Following the same tradition, the Great Britain team decided on their assembly the night before their big race:

1. Derek Redmond, the then 400m national record holder, who finished in the seventh place in 45.67s in the semi-final Heat 1 and as a result failed to make it through to the 400m finals, would run the first leg against Andrew Valmon.
2. John Regis, a 200m specialist and European champion in the event, who finished in fifth place in 20.52s in Heat 2 of the semi-finals and as a result failed to gain a place on the 200m final list, would run the second leg against the more experienced Quincy Watts.
3. Kriss Akabusi, the 400m hurdler who took bronze at the games in 47.86s, would battle against Danny Everett.
4. Roger Black, who clocked 44.42s to take the silver medal at the games, would be the anchor.

That was the assembly. The fastest man would anchor the baton home. Agreed. Good night lads. And off they went to their rooms. Roger Black and Kriss Akabusi shared the same room, and Derek Redmond and John Regis in one room.

Then came the 'unthinkable' conversation (extracted from Derek Redmond's presentation[13]) between Kriss Akabusi and Roger Black, unknown to the others[14]:

Kriss: Roger, if you want to get the best out of me, put me in the last leg.

Roger: What?

Kriss: If you want to get the best out of me.

Roger: Why do you think you can run the last leg. Explain.

*A leader should **sell** a realistic vision*

Kriss: I ran the last leg in the heat in 44.2s, in third gear. I've got more petrol, probably two gears to go. You give me that baton ... and I would bring that gold medal. Mark my word, I will bring you the gold medal.

Roger: Let us assume you run the last leg. Where am I supposed to go, because I have to run the last leg? (after a brief pause) OK, I've got it. I'll run the first leg?

Kriss: But why run the first leg? Why not run the third?

A leader should be analytical

Roger: I am the second fastest man in the world in 400m. We know the fastest man in the world is Antonio Pettigrew from America. There is a 99.99% chance they're going to stick him in the last leg. And so if you stick me in the first leg, after the first lap, we would have the lead. That is unusual in any major championship.

---

[13] http://www.derekredmond.com/speaking.asp
[14] Ibid

Roger and Kriss had agreed on their **vision**, clearly defined their **roles** and how the **Land of Promise** (the gold medal) could be reached. However, there was an important gap left to fill. It was a 4 by 400m race and not a 2 by 400m race. They therefore had the task to **sell** the **vision** to the other members as well as convince them to **own** the **vision**.

In essence, a deep sense of **respect** exist (to date) between the four athletes and a fifth, Mark Richardson (on standby for any eventuality such as injury). On their next meeting, Kriss and Roger **sold** their vision to their colleagues. Derek and John's roles had to be defined in order to get them to fully become a part of the shared leadership process towards achieving the vision:

Good leadership is about stimulating others to participate in the decis-ion-making

- Derek would run the second leg to extend the lead if Roger succeeded in his quest or at least keep a close distance behind Quincy Watts.
- John would run the third leg closely behind the American to intimidate him with his bulky stature.

Among them, the GB men's 4 by 400m team built a new **team** quite different from that of the previous day. They identified and successfully **sold** their **vision**. They positioned themselves for the **Promised Land** and **how to get there**. Their coach (the **formal leader**) must have been **supportive** of the presentation by the **informal leaders** in the team to thrive.

'Would this gamble pay off?' The British commentator, at the Games, asked the million dollar question.

The commentator had every reason to doubt the GB 4 by 400m team's plan, for by all counts the US Men's 4 by 400m team had the edge over their British counterparts. According to Derek's analysis[15] of the individual 400m personal best times, the Time Difference between the two teams were:

GB Team	PB*	US Team	PB*	TD**
Roger Black	44.36s	Andrew Valmon	44.21s	0.15s
Derek Redmond	44.50s	Quincy Watts	43.91s	0.59s
John Regis	45.56s	Danny Everett	43.97s	1.59s
Kriss Akabusi	44.93s	Antonio Pettigrew	44.17s	0.76s

PB* = Personal Best; TD** = Time Difference

Derek's analysis suggested that the GB Team were not only significantly slower on each leg, but they were also in principle 3.09 seconds behind the US Team, equating to at least 27m behind the latter.

The final 4 by 400m men's race time arrived, and all the first leg athletes, representing the qualified countries, assembled in their lanes. The athletes got on their marks, got set, and the start gun was fired, resulting[16] in:

Roger Black delivered

Roger Black securing a slight lead over the Americans to hand the baton to Derek Redmond;

Derek Redmond delivered

Derek Redmond ran his hardest to maintain the lead for well over 300m before Quincy Watts slightly edged him towards the finish line;

John Regis delivered

John Regis stuck closely behind Danny Everett, ensuring the gap between him and the American never grew any bigger; and

15 http://www.youtube.com/watch?v=BXN7fv-APRQ&NR=1&feature=endscreen
16 http://www.youtube.com/watch?v=1PEdNfnRbAc

Kriss Akabusi, on receiving the baton from John Regis, gave Antonio Pettigrew the chase maintaining nearly the same gap his teammate had worked hard for. After 300m, Kriss stepped in-between lanes 1 and 2 to position himself to attempt a neck-to-neck race against Pettigrew. The stadium roared at the surprise challenge the 400m hurdler bronze medalist gave the 1991 world's fastest 400m man in the home straight. They both had determination in their eyes but a few metres to the finish line, Kriss Akabusi passed Antonio Pettigrew to give Team GB the gold he had promised.

Kriss Akabusi delivered

At the end of the day, all the GB 4 by 400m Men's Team members carried out their shared responsibilities as promised. After 2 minutes 57.54s, their collective **team effort** got them to become the 1991 4 by 400m **World Champions**, setting:

1. A **New National Record**
2. A **New European Record**
3. A **New Commonwealth Record**, and
4. A **New Area Record**

The above feat was achieved through identifying a clear **vision** to benefit the entire team, **team-building**, **respect** for the team members, **effective communication** and **listening skills**, acknowledging the core **values of democracy** to foster **collective participation** of the team members, stimulating **participatory brainstorming** for a **collective decision-making**, recognizing the possible cooperation between **informal** and **formal leaders**, and the like. These **leadership characteristics** are latently seated in each of us.

Two funda-mental concepts of leadership: formal and informal

The above scenario demonstrates that democracy and leadership are a part of our everyday life, whether we are conscious of it or not. The leadership characteristics exhibited by the 1991 Osaka IAAF GB 4 X 400m men's team are reminiscent of the elements of **formal** and **informal leadership**. The following section further defines and elaborates what formal and informal leadership entails.

4.0 Formal and informal leadership

There are two fundamental concepts of leadership, namely **formal** and **informal** leadership. A formal leader is one who has been formally appointed/recruited/elected to a recognized position of high authority and therefore holds an institutional power over a group. A **formal leader** holds an official position such as CEO, CFO, Vice President, Head Teacher, UN Secretary General, Prime Minister, Dean of a faculty, Commander in Chief, etc. However, among the group the formal leader leads, there may be one or more **key influential figures** who have a strong influence over the group members. This *key influential person* is sometimes the one the group members turn to for emotional and social **support**. S/he maintains a **two-way communication** line with the group members, compared to the formal leader who might take a **one-way communication** approach if s/he is task-oriented and therefore is apt to give *high directives* to get the job done. Depending on the expertise of the **key influential person**, the group members sometimes seeks her/his support for further clarifications with the task.

An informal leader influences the group

Although the *key influential person* has no officially recognized leadership title on the organizational chart, s/he has the influential power to get the task done, instigate a boycott; encourage a strike; stage a demonstration to demand salary raise, kill a project's vision, etc. Such a powerful and influential person is a recognized leader among her/his peers (the group). S/he is an **informal leader**. For example, when I was a young boy, my grandfather saw himself as the Head of the House (**formal leader** by default) and on several occasions commanded me to do things. On all of *those several occasions*, I defiantly refused to do anything he had harshly commanded. At the end of the day, it was only my grandmother's strategic **informal leadership** approach that got me to execute the tasks the Head of the House had commanded.

Regardless of the **formal leader's** leadership role, the group members connect better with the **informal leader** than with the former. The **informal leader** appears charismatic, outgoing and supportive to keep her/his relationship with her/his peers. Under certain circumstances it is worth for the **formal leader** to strike a good relationship with the **informal leader**, who is in the position to share with the former the core needs of the group of employees. However, such marriages do not always last. For instance, if the formal leader is inclined to believe that the informal leader's influence over the group has the potential to undermine the formal leader's **vision**, the latter may exercise her/his power and rights to remove the informal leader on the premise of protecting the **vision**.

The formal and informal leader can explore a ground to cooperate

Informal leadership can be seen as an important element of organizational behaviour (Weiss, 1978; Han, 1983; Robins and Zirinsky, 1996; Doloff, 1999). Compared to the vast worth of information available on formal leadership (French and Raven, 1959; Wheelan, 1996; Bass, 1999; Bass and Steidlmeier, 1999; McShane and von Glinow, 2000), only little research has been done in the area. This presents a significant gap in literature that makes it difficult to compare formal and informal leadership paradigms in order to critically analyse what an ideal leadership process is.

There is limited information on informal leadership

4.1 Defining leadership

4.1.1 What is leadership?

Leadership is a shared responsi-bility

Serving as a leader entails being seen as a role model, supervisor, director, motivator, counsellor, supporter, coach, teacher, manager, guide, etc. The activities that are embedded in leadership are a shared responsibility in the sense that the leader partners with the followers in order to gain their full cooperation. Leadership can be both a daunting task and exciting. The success of good leadership is a function of how well the leader channels her/his leadership skills to benefit her/himself and her/his follower(s) (community, staff, environment, organisation, nation, etc.).

Leadership is about tapping into resources

Leadership may be described in the context of successfully harnessing available resources (*you*, others, the environment, human dignity, democracy, culture, community, etc.) for the achievement of both human and societal development. This definition presents a fundamental understanding of what leadership is about. We can infer from such a fundamental description that a leader is *one who seeks the developmental interest of others as well as the society or the environment with which s/he interacts.* Dictionary definitions of leadership, often, fail to make enough sense. The Collins English Dictionary[17], for example, defines **leadership** as:

1. The position or function of a leader
2. The period during which a person occupies the position of leader
    a. the ability to lead;
    b. (as modifier) such as leadership qualities
3. The leaders as a group of a party, union

Considering the broadness of the subject-matter, such definitions as above provide very little information.

---

[17] http://www.collinsdictionary.com/dictionary/english/leadership?showCookiePolicy=true

Leadership is a broad field. As such the definitions of leadership are diverse. There are quite a number of definitions of leadership in literature. As there is no one universal definition for leadership, the subject may be derived based on the circumstance or situation in which a leadership role is required to achieve a particular goal. For instance, a functioning leadership paradigm in one football club may not necessarily function in another club in the same community.

In certain environments, particularly in the military, leadership is *Obey before you complain!* With such leadership concept, can you lead your friends and still remain friends with them? In other circles, leadership is about *Do it my way. Finito!* Are these the kind of tones you would want to be representative or descriptive of your leadership style? In this respect, rather than be limited to dictionary or subjective or generic definitions of the subject-matter, this section of the book encourages you to derive the definition of leadership in your own words.

4.1.2 Defining leadership in your own words

In this section, the following seven steps will help you take a practical or an active approach to derive a definition of **leadership** in your own words:

Step One:

Think through your answers to the following questions:

1. How many times have you said to yourself: *This or that leader could have done things this way or that way to easily achieve this or that expected sets of goals for the benefit of the community?*

2. Do you find yourself being asked to lead others but have no clue on which foot to begin?

Step Two:

Read about other leaders (dedicated and devoted people making a difference in other people's lives as well as in both their communities and the global society) and pay keen attention to how these leaders described/describe leadership in their own words. Remember to always keep an open mind as you read about their leadership styles. Read also about the once held-in-high-esteem leaders who made bad decisions that robbed them of respect, and extract lessons from their mistakes.

Step Three:

Give your written response to the following:

Assess and write about 10 leaders you admire

1. Name 10 leaders and what you admire about each of them.
2. How are these 10 leaders different from others?
3. Given their approach to leadership and achievements, how do you think they would collectively perceive or define **leadership**?

Step Four:

Would the collective definition of leadership, modelled on the leadership styles of the 10 leaders you admire (in Step Three) work for you and your community? Remember that you are unique and therefore your personality and core strengths may be different compared to the ten leaders you admire. Your circumstance, the resources around you, your core targets, etc., may also be quite different from those of your role models. As you brainstorm for your personalised definition of leadership, you should also decide what your leadership approach would look like as this has to have a place in your definition of the subject-matter.

Step Five:

Answer, in writing, the following questions to help you identify and generate core **single keywords** (such as achiever, insightful, persistent, innovative, trustworthy, honest, cheerful, enthusiastic, funny) or **keyword phrases** (such as goal-oriented, sense of humour, interpersonal skills, take-charge person, goal-chaser, good listener, good communicator, entrepreneurial characteristics, eloquent speaker) to feature in your definition of leadership.

1. What are your core strengths? Describe your core strengths in terms of keywords or keyword phrases.
2. In which areas in your community or organisation do you want to make a difference?
3. What (characteristics, traits, etc.) makes you a motivational or inspirational powerhouse?
4. What are the ten main things you dislike in leadership approaches that you are familiar with?

A leader's inherent and/or developed characteristics can influence her/his leadership approach

Step Six:

Self-assess yourself as to whether the **keywords** (personality traits and/or developed abilities) below can be associated with your ability to lead others:

Integrity: Are you consistently honest, reliable, trustworthy, etc.?

Participative: Do you share information, consult with those you lead and involve others in the decision-making processes?

Goal-oriented: Do you set challenging goals and strive to achieve them by empowering others to improve performance?

Diplomatic: Do you accord others with respect regardless of their sex, religion, colour of skin, social status, etc.?

Democratic: Are you fair to your fellow humankind regardless of their ethnic background or nationality? Do human dignity, human rights, etc., have a place in your personality?

Self-confidence: Are you self-confident and ever-ready to admit and learn from your mistakes? Are you confident enough to say a bold *I am sorry for offending you by my poor choice of words* and to avoid a very bigotry approach that often sounds like *If you find my words offensive, sorry?*

Cognitive ability: Does your level of intelligence allow you to process information quickly and deal with changes in your community?

Respect: Are you civil towards others in your community or do you look down on others just because you think you are better than they are?

Supportive: Do you lead and still remain friends with the people you lead?

Directive: Is your leadership behaviour descriptive of implementing regulations, rules or guidelines for what is expected to be accomplished?

Self-esteem: Do you channel your self-esteem nature to help others grow? Are you the type who would say to another *this topic is in my professional field and so keep off that turf until you've read extensively about the subject?* It is noteworthy that intimidating-style use of your high self-esteem can be seen as an attempt to shatter the self-esteem of others.

Motivation powerhouse: Do people look up to you for inspiration to enable them to move forward?

Community-centred: Are you focused on helping your community thrive and not only focused on what-is-in-it-for-me?

Good listener: Are you a good listener or do you always/usually like to have the last word?

Good communication skills: Do you possess the ability to both communicate effectively and listen attentively?

Step Seven:

Your decision to fine-tune your personality in order to become a people's person, a better and more effective leader, implies that you plan to rewrite the definition of leadership. In this regard, you must define leadership in such a way that it embeds your fine-tuned personality and good approach to leading others whilst remaining their good friend.

Refine your personality to position you for leadership

Rewrite the definition of leadership to be characteristic of your nature of driving the lives of others and your community forward.

Seeking feedback on your definition

As leadership is about leading others to thrive, it is worth to consider seeking the thoughts of others about your definition of leadership. This exercise is important in that you are starting by involving others in your definitions. In effect, you are stimulating participatory leadership by seeking a collective leadership. Thus, the following are worth considering:

- Define **leadership** based on the information you have drafted across Steps One and Seven.
- Email or send your definition of **leadership** to 10 people of different age groups and ask for their honest feedback.
- Does your definition, based on the feedback, include elements of democratic leadership?

Get others to have an input in your leadership definition

4.2 The Great Man Theory of Leadership

The Great Man Theory was developed by Thomas Carlyle in the 1940s, on the premise that **great men** or heroes greatly impacted their societies and left significant historical footprints on other landscapes. The theory suggests that Great Men are born leaders. In May 1789, Napoleon Bonaparte wrote to Pasquale Paoli, a Corsican leader (McLynn, 1998):

Napoleon implied he had been born at a time of need for a strong leader

'*As the nation was perishing I was born. Thirty thousand Frenchmen were vomited on to our shores, drowning the throne of liberty in waves of blood. Such was the odious sight which was the first to strike me.*'

In the above message, Napoleon appeared to suggest that he had been **born** at the time when a perishing nation probably needed a new **leader**. This, among several similar questions from so-called heroes, prompts the question:

Were Napoleon Bonaparte, Alexander the Great, Julius Caesar, Otto von Bismarck, Kim Il Sung, and other so-called Great Men made or born to lead, in agreement with the theory?

A quick journey into chronicling Napoleon's conquest would reveal him both as a hero (by the society that made or birth*ed* him as a leader) and villain (by the societies he scarred). Yet, his leadership trends would provide a study material, in terms of an element of Understanding Leadership, by schools of thought.

As the history of the so-called Great Men of Leadership is beyond the scope of this book, we will only visit a few of the significant paths of Napoleon in order to question whether leaders are made or born. Books on Napoleonic wars have attempted to provide insights into understanding leadership in general. It is worth questioning as to whether the leadership style that yielded a General Napoleon's bloody military triumphs intertwines with that of a postcoronation branded mafia-styled Emperor Napoleon. Leaders the likes of Muhammad Ali of Egypt and Austrian-born dictator Adolf Hitler admired Napoleon and his leadership style so much that they sought to emulate him. Given the fact that the vast majority of the so-called Great Men were warmongers and dictators, and essentially adopted each other's leadership style, the question remains as to whether leaders in this category were born or made.

Like-minded leaders influence one another

Adolf Hitler saw Napoleon as a great leader, great man, one who built empires and one whose leadership skills ushered him as King over Italy, Emperor of France, and a Great Warrior. These characteristics likely shaped Hitler's personality and ambition in terms of making himself powerful, the most feared, and expanding his territories. When Hitler's Germany occupied France in the Second World War, the dictator paid homage to Napoleon's tomb at Les Invalides to demonstrate his love for his dead hero. In comprehending the scars that are reminiscent of Hitler's authoritative leadership, for example, would a leader Hitler recognized as a Great Man be seen or accepted as same by others?

Was Hitler's hero everybody's hero?

Men, arguably, wrote the Great Man of Leadership theory and similar literature to demonstrate the male-factor dominance in the past worlds. Such bias attitudes against women also culminated in men's past dominance in the book publishing industry. Were there Great Women of Leadership? Historically, yes. Born without any leadership and military skills, Queen Victoria became the commander of the British army and the nation's leader who sent out dispatches to *successfully* force colonial rules on many countries now called Commonwealth states. Unlike Napoleon who trained in the army and had track records of military tactics showcased by the many wars he won, Victoria knew nothing about military leadership. Was Victoria made by society or a God-gifted leader?

There were also great women of leadership

In 1900, when British governor Frederick Hodgson demanded that the Ashantis of Ghana hand him their ancestral dynastic Golden Stool, the Ashanti men lost speech instantly. Hodgson had wanted to sit on the stool simply to demonstrate the British power. The legendary Queen Mother Nana Yaa Asantewaa[18] of Ejisuhene, Ashanti Region, in today's Ghana, raised her voice above her countrymen and dared the governor:

Nana Yaa Asantewaa was a great woman of courage and leadership

'Now I see that some of you fear to go forward to fight for our king. If it [was] in the brave days of Osei Tutu, Okomfo Anokye, and Opoku Ware, chiefs would not sit down to see their king to be taken away without firing a shot. No European could have dared speak to chiefs of Asante in the way the governor spoke to you this morning. Is it true that the bravery of Asante is no more? I cannot believe it. It cannot be! I must say this: if you, the men of Asante, will not go forward, then we will. We, the women, will. I shall call upon my fellow women. We will fight! We will fight till the last of us falls in the battlefields'[19] (Addy, 1960; Kyeretwie, 1964; Myatt, 1966)

Courage may be an element of leadership

The 60-year-old grandmother Nana Yaa Asantewaa led a tactical army of 5000 in what became historically known as the last battle against colonial British[20]. Having won the battle against the better-equipped British colonial army to preserve her community's dignity, Nana Yaa Asantewaa was seen as an inherently courageous Great Woman of Leadership (Addy, 1960; Kyeretwie, 1964; Myatt, 1966).

4.3 Trait Theory of Leadership

Defined in terms of '*...integrated patterns of individual traits that reflect a range of individual differences and foster consistent leadership effectiveness across a range of group and organizational domains* (Zaccaro *et al.*, 2004), the Trait Theory of

---

[18] http://en.wikipedia.org/wiki/Yaa_Asantewaa
[19] Ibid.
[20] Ibid

Leadership remains the oldest approach to characterising (see Table 1) and identifying potential leaders who are likely to succeed or those that might fail. Its associated theoretical models are sometimes used in an attempt to assess whether a leader would succeed with reference to traits demonstrated by past and present leaders.

The Trait Theory of Leadership is a metric for leadership effectiveness

Table 1: Personality Traits and Skills (Stodgill, 1974)

Traits	Skills
Adaptable to situations	Clever (intelligent)
Alert to social environment	Conceptually skills
Ambitions and achievement-oriented	Creative
Assertive	Diplomatic and tactful
Cooperative	Fluent in speaking
Decisive	Knowledgeable about group task
Dependable	Organised (administrative ability)
Dominant (desire to influence others)	Persuasive
Persistent	Socially skills
Self-confident	
Tolerant to stress	
Willing to assume responsibility	

In 1869, Galton suggested via his hypothesis that studying the personality traits of individuals can help predict how effective and successful a leader is likely to be (Derue *et al*, 2011). From Galton's hypothesis (1869) follow that:

Galton's hypothesis suggests that leadership is an inherent ability

- Leadership is a unique ability that is possessed by certain extraordinary individuals, and their opinions and decisions are capable of bringing about radical changes

- The unique attributes of (these) leaders is part of their genetic makeup, implying that leadership hereditary.

The above notion is characteristic of the dispute that stems from the assumption that the so-called Great Men were inherently born to lead. Up to the early twentieth century, leadership was thought of as a **male quality** due to the fact that most of the Great Men of Leadership were war-mongering heroes. However, the fact that the legendary Queen Mother Nana Yaa Asantewaa successfully battled Victoria's colonial army to preserve her community's dynastic stool may suggest that the Great Man theory presents a flawed conclusion that *only men are born leaders.*

1. Distinguish between formal and informal leadership.
2. Identify situations in which formal and informal leadership may be suitably applied.
3. What risks do formal and informal leaders share?
4. How can a formal leader benefit from an informal leader, and vice versa?
5. Recalling Chapters 1 – 3, discuss as to whether there can be a potential balance between formal and informal leadership that can culminate in a democratic leadership process. You are encouraged to use example scenarios to illustrate your argument.
6. Define leadership, in general.
7. Compare and contrast the following definitions of leadership:

    a. *'Leadership is a process of social influence in which one person is able to enlist the aid and support of others in the accomplishment of a common task'* — (Chemers, 2002) and

    b. *'Leadership is ultimately about creating a way for people to contribute to making something extraordinary happen'* — (Kouzes and Posner, 2007).

8. How has the Great Man theory influenced your understanding of leadership?
9. Describe the Trait Theory of Leadership in terms of its strengths/advantages, limitations and implications. Draw a tangible conclusion.
10. In comprehending the scars that are reminiscent of Hitler's authoritative leadership, for example, would a leader Hitler recognised as a Great Man be seen or accepted as same by others? If your response is yes or no, give reasons for your answer.

References

Addy, E. A (1960): *Ghana History for Primary Schools*, Book 2. Longmans, London.

Bass, B. M (1990a): Bass and Stogdill's *Handbook of Leadership: Theory, Research, and Managerial Applications* (3rd ed.). New York: Free Press.

Bass, B. M. and P Steidlmeier (1999): *Ethics, character, and authentic transformational leadership behaviour.* Leadership quarterly, 10 (2), pp. 181-217.

Derue, D. S, J.D Nahrgang, N Wellman and S.E Humphrey (2011): *Trait and behavioural theories - of leadership: An integration and: meta-analytic test of their relative validity.* Personnel Psychology, 4(1), 7-52.

Doloff, P. G (1999): *Beyond the organization chart.* Across the board, 36 (2), pp. 43-47.

French, J.R.P and B Raven (1959): *The Bases of Social Power.* In D. Cartwright (Ed.), Studies in Social Power, pp. 150-167. Ann Arbor: University of Michigan Institute for Social Research.

Galton, F (1869): *Hereditary genius.* New York: Appleton.

Han, P.E (1983): *The Informal Organization You've Got to Live With.* Supervisory Management, 28(10), pp. 25-28.

Kyeretwie, K.O.B (1964): *Ashanti Heroes.* Oxford University Press, London.

Lord, R. G, C.L De Vader and G.M Alliger (1986): *A meta-analysis of the relation between personality traits and leadership perceptions: An application of validity generalization procedures.* Journal of Applied Psychology, 71, pp. 402–410.

McLynn, F (1998): *Napoleon: A Biography.* London: Pimlico.

McShane, S.L and M.A Von Glinow (2000): *Organizational behavior.* Boston, MA: Irwin McGraw-Hill.

Myatt, F (1966): *The Golden Stool, Ashanti 1900.* William Kimber Publishers, London.

Nieuwazny, A: *Napoleon and Polish Identity*. History Today, May 1998, Vol. 48, Nos. 5, pp. 50–55.

Robbins, B and D Zirinsky (1996): *Growing into leadership: Profiles from a 'good' department*. English journal, 85(5), pp. 34-39.

Stogdill, R.M (1974): *Handbook of leadership: A survey of the literature*, New York: Free Press.

Weiss, A.J (1978): *Surviving and succeeding in the "political" organization: Becoming a leader*. Supervisory Management, 23(8), 27.

Wheelan, S.A (1996): *The role of informal member leaders in a system containing formal leaders*. Small group research, 27(1), pp. 33-55.

Zaccaro, S.J, C Kemp and P Bader (2004): *Leader traits and attributes*. The nature of leadership. pp. 101-124. Thousand Oaks, CA, US: Sage Publications, Inc.

Chapter 5

PARADIGMS OF LEADERSHIP

5.0 Leadership theories

Leaders are unique individuals whose leadership styles may be defined by their inherent personality traits, characters or acquired skills, shaped by both the people they lead and the conditions of the situation or environment. Leadership comes in a number of forms (such as political leadership, civil rights leadership, organisational leadership, business management leadership) that may require different leadership approaches. There are several types of leadership theories, such as participatory, bureaucratic, transformational, autocratic, functional, supportive, laissez-faire, task-oriented, contingency-based, transactional, servant, environment, democratic, achievement-oriented, charismatic, directive, people-oriented leaderships, situational, etc. However, the scope of this book is to essentially encourage democratic leadership processes. Acknowledging the fact that different circumstances or situations expect leadership to coevolve with the changing functional requirements of the followers and/or society, the subsequent sections will focus on the following four leadership theories as they can be adopted in combination to stimulate democratic leadership processes:

Several types of leadership styles exist

1. Participatory leadership
2. Transformational leadership
3. Situational leadership
4. Contingency-based leadership

This book focuses on four theories of leadership

5.1 Participatory leadership

Considered sustainable and an empowering tool to develop success-oriented organisational structure, transform business for growth, promote democratic change in the community, etc., the meaning of Participatory Leadership can be derived from the following core characteristics:

Tantamount to a democratic form of leadership

- Inculcates the culture of respect for others;
- Encourages active involvement of all project group members;
- Involves all members of the project team or group and offers them the opportunity to contribute thoughts to identify essential sub-goals towards the final goal;
- Encourages collaboration between team or community members to develop procedures or strategies to achieve the goal/vision;
- Seeks general consensus for decision-making;
- Recognises individual member's talent and skills for the betterment of the project;
- Promotes balanced opportunity for all parties (leader and follower);
- Explores deepened individual and collective learning through knowledge or expertise sharing to stimulate individual or group development and growth;
- Encourages shared responsibility for appropriate action to achieve the goal;
- Focuses and taps into the inner resources of all members, an element of inclusiveness that suggests an advanced form of *democratic* leadership;
- Etc.

Can stimulate community growth

The elements or characteristics of **participatory leadership** listed above can culminate in the processes required for the developments of **leadership** and a **community**. One essential component of the participative leader is that the leader serves as a facilitator (or mentor) rather than acting on an authoritative platform, delegating or commanding tasks about. As the term implies, participatory leadership is about involving all team members or individuals to participate in the leadership processes for the common good of achieving the goal. This approach is seen as democratic as it encourages the voice of all the members in order to formulate decisions derived from a consensus or collective contributions.

5.1.1 Theoretical background

According to the Lewin's study (Lewin *et al*, 1939), *Participative Leadership is generally the most effective leadership style. This is because, just as with democratic leaders, a Participative Leader offers mentorship to the (project) group members as well as participates directly like a group member.*

A participative leader is seen as a mentor

Acknowledging the leadership inherent in each follower, the participatory leader is part of the team and taps into the inner resources (talent and skills) of each member for the development of the business organisation or charity organization or community. This enables individual members to not only have their voices in the project, but also have the confidence to express their innovative ideas, etc. Besides identifying and exploring the strengths of the subordinates, the participative leadership approach enables the leader to not only identify the weaknesses and strengths of the team members but also to provide appropriate support (mentorship). This leadership style transforms all the members of the community or organisation into great assets.

A participative leader seeks the collective voices of the team members

Unlike other leadership styles (such as authoritative) that place power into the hands of one person (the leader), a leader who adopts a participatory leadership style encourages participatory brainstorming for collective decision-making. A participatory brainstorming session can reveal strengths, weaknesses, opportunities and threats (SWOT), and solicit collective strategies on how best to reach the goal or core goals. This follows that a project challenge can be approached from various angles, making room for different possibilities to be explored to derive the ideal solution. This approach to shared functions, democratic or collective leadership or governing is demonstrated by President Obama's commitment to '...*making this the most open and participatory administration in history. That begins with taking your questions and comments, inviting you to join online events with White House officials, and giving you a way to engage with your government on the issues that matter the most.*'[21]

The Obama administration encourages participatory leadership

Participatory grants equal opportunity to the people

The Obama administration's approach to participatory leadership presents a window of opportunity to enable the people to make their voices heard on tax and other important issues. The suitability of the participative leadership style is oriented on the fact that when a vision is ambiguous in presentation, the leader participates actively in order to give greater clarity to how best the vision can be understood by the followers or community. Pertinent queries that seek in-depth clarification about Obama's political manifesto or platform can be submitted in various ways for the President to address or the people can arrange to visit the White House. As the subordinates are, in principle, autonomous and have a strong need for control, the participative leader presents a positive impact by involving the followers in organizing the task to encourage a collective decision (Northouse, 2010).

5.1.2 Classification of participative leadership

With reference to its basic platform for leadership, participative leaders can be classified into the following three groups (Pride *et al*, 2012):

[21] www.whitehouse.gov/engage (Last Accessed: 09.01.2013)

1. **Consultative**: The leader actively discusses the tasks with the subordinates or followers while retaining the final word.
2. **Consensus**: The leader encourages collective involvement in the brainstorming session in order to reach a consensus for the final collective decision.
3. **Democratic**: The leader actually puts the final authority in the hands of the subordinates or group or followers.

Participatory leadership is a platform for shared leadership

Subordinates under participative leadership are able to work effectively because they are motivated and empowered to implement their own decisions for the betterment of the project. The participative leader must develop coaching, negotiation, collaboration and communication skills to be effective.

5.1.3 Advantages and disadvantages of participative leadership

In order to guide the enthusiastic participative leader to plan her/his leadership style, it is paramount to be aware of some of the prominent advantages and disadvantages listed in Table 2.

Table 2: Advantages and disadvantages of participatory leadership

Advantages	Disadvantages
Subordinates may feel that their ideas are important, making them to feel more committed to changes and decision-making in which they have participated.[22]	The participative approach to leadership assumes a considerable commonality of interest between the leaders and subordinates, *whereas this might not necessarily be the case*.[23]

---

[22] Ricketts and Ricketts (2011).
[23] *Ibid.*

Entrusted to make competent decisions, the team members develop greater sense of self-esteem and belief in their abilities. This leads to earning respect for their inputs.[24]	Some individual members in the group may be uninterested, resulting to apathy towards the project.[25]
The combined knowledge and experiences of the subordinates usually exceed those of the leader.[26]	Followers might perceive the participative approach as an attempt to manipulate them.[27]
Problems that subordinates work on as a team often lead to new ideas, created as a result of the interpersonal exchanges and discussions of various options.[28]	The participative approach assumes that the group members have the necessary knowledge and skills to implement and participate in the decision making process, *which they may not have.*[29]
Participatory leadership style boosts human dignity and promotes respect for all.	Some leaders feel uncomfortable using a participative style because of their personality type.[30]
This approach to leadership encourages shared ownership, stimulating subordinates to always invest their best efforts in the project.	Some leaders hesitate to use participative leadership for fear that they will lose control over their group members.[31]
This leadership approach offers an ideal managerial method for small and medium-sized enterprises and large corporations as it solicits the involvement of all the employees whose input can yield growth.	The trend to involve everyone in brainstorming sessions can be time-consuming.

---

[24] Ricketts and Ricketts (2011).
[25] *Ibid.*
[26] *Ibid.*
[27] *Ibid.*
[28] *Ibid.*
[29] *Ibid.*
[30] *Ibid.*
[31] *Ibid.*

As an involved leadership mechanism, it is more easy to implement new policies. This is because the derivation of new organizational policies takes into consideration the collective voices of the subordinates. Unlike other authoritative-oriented leadership styles that isolate the subordinates, the participatory leadership mode gets the subordinates to participate in formulating new policies that they indirectly approve.	
The participatory leadership style encourages employee retention. When employees are recognized for their input and made to count themselves as part of the organization's success, they feel encouraged to stay with the organization.	

5.2 Transformational leadership

When the then little known Illinois senator Barack Obama chanted his 2008 Presidential bid campaign slogan, *Yes, we can!*, he triggered enthusiasm in the youth, minorities, the underprivileged, the middle-class, women, and the domain that has always felt marginalized by the previous political systems. He got the United States and the world to pause for a moment and question as to whether he was serious or joking about his quest for the White House. Many hurdles stood in his way: his name is Barack Hussein Obama, he is black – half-Kenyan and half-American, had little relevant experience for the highest executive position in the United States of America and had a controversial spiritual leader. In spite of all those challenges, Obama implied that it was time to put racial boundaries out of focus. The most asked question was whether the United States of America was

The Yes, we can! slogan changed the status quo in US politics

Transform-ational leadership is about overcoming barriers to bring change

ready to elect the nation's first black president in November 2008.

Yes, we can!

A leader must inspire her/his followers

Obama **inspired** a large segment of the US population into believing in themselves — that with determination and perseverance they can achieve their dreams. His 2008 campaign speeches, advocating for change, were essentially motivational speaking that positioned him as an evolving Transformational Leader. By presenting that he understands their pains and challenges, cares about their needs and plans to bring change (transformation) to Washington, Obama successfully garnered millions of followers both at home and abroad.

As evidenced in Obama's approach, the core message of a Transformational Leader is essentially *I care about you and want you to succeed.* This is embedded in his message that *I want you to have a shot at the American Dream.*

5.2.1 Theoretical background

By definition, a transformational leader is one who recognizes and taps into the needs and sense of identity of her/his target followers in order to position her/himself as an inspiring figure or role model for the group.

Transformational leadership is not limited to political leadership. In a business organization, a **leader** empowers the employees or colleagues to take ownership for their work and to give it their all as if they own the organization. In this respect, the leader examines the strengths and weaknesses of the followers to better their performance.

In his research on political leaders, James MacGregor Burns, who first introduced the concept of transformational leadership, gave the following definition (Burns, 2003): *'Transformational Leadership is a process in which leaders and followers help each other to advance to a higher level of morale and motivation.'*

Burn's theory (Burns, 2003; Barker, *et al.*, 2006) of transformational leadership seeks to address aspects of an organisation to thrive, stimulate enthusiasm in the group (employees or subordinates) and identify the values the subordinates can bring into their responsibilities. In order for a transformational leader to demonstrate that s/he cares about the follower and wants the latter to succeed, the leader is expected to map her/his leadership approach through the 4 general steps in Table 3:

There are four general steps in transformational leadership

Table 3: Transformational leadership matrix

STEP 1	THE VISION	1. In order to inspire, energise, excite and convert potential followers, a transformational leader (and her/his core organising team) must first develop a clear vision.
		2. Whether the vision is solely developed by the transformational leader or in collaboration with her/his core organising team, s/he must not only buy into the vision, but also get the team member to also own it.
		3. The leader will take an **Inspirational Motivation** approach to articulate the vision to both appeal to and inspire the followers. This aspect is a core element of transformational leadership.
STEP 2	SELLING THE VISION	1. The leader must be able to sell the vision to the core target group.
		2. If the leader wishes to see

		exponential growth in the number of her/his followers, then selling her/his vision never ends. S/he must constantly sell the vision at every given opportunity. During the 2008 presidential campaign, Obama both honoured and solicited invitations to appear on prime Talk Shows. He used the platform to chip in his vision. This helped increase the number of his followers.
		3. The leader's personality and integrity is part of the total package. Any scandal or unscrupulous behaviour or past history that potentially exposes the leader's reputation to public scrutiny can be a career or vision killer. This essentially follows that the leader must be an **Idealized Influence**.
STEP 3	PROGRESSING	**1.** As a transformational leader, you are the one with the vision. As such, you are the one to lead the way to the **promised destination**. This third step is about exploring possible ways to get the followers to the destination. During his 2008 presidential elections, Obama's task was to show which route would be feasible to **change** the status quo or the *business politics as usual* in Washington DC.
		2. As the way forward may not be obvious to the team members, the transformational leader must assure her/his followers that the **journey is an ongoing process**. This aspect is very important in that the leader must warn her/his followers of any inevitable dangers or challenges ahead.
STEP 4	LEADING	**1.** The fourth step is for the leader to interconnect the vision, selling the vision, and progressing. The transformational leader must remain visible, reachable or

available. During his early months or years after winning the 2008 elections, US President Obama attended a number of Town Hall format meetings (face-to-face and via the YouTube platform) and honoured a few invitations to appear on Talk Shows. This strategically positioned him in front of the core followers, as well as inspired future followers for 2012. This approach of continued efforts to inspire is strategic for sustained commitment. This is a demonstration of an important element of transformational leadership called **Individualised Consideration**, in which the leader seeks to address the interests of her/his followers.

2. US Secretary of State Hillary Clinton said in a CNN interview with Jessica Yellin that, President Obama pays attention to details and that he reads proposals or reports thoroughly and often grant audience to the authors to debate alternatives, etc.[32] A transformational leader listens attentively and s/he remains thoughtful and supportive.

3. A transformational leader must have an unwavering personality in the midst of challenges, without giving room to flip-flopping or making excuses. President Obama, during his first term in office, once called on fellow US citizens to urge the congressional representatives that they (the people) had voted into the House, to act appropriately by working together (bi-partisanship) in decision-making necessary to drive the country's economy forward. This approach is **collaborative leadership** (Gardiner, 2006), characteristic of a transformational leader

---

[32] http://www.youtube.com/watch?v=D3fHppBHGUo (Last Access: 10.12.2012)

	in the face of challenges. The extent Obama went to solicit the cooperation of US citizens is a democratic element of transformational leadership known as **Intellectual Stimulation**.

5.2.2 Characteristics of a transformational leader

We can deduce from Burn's theory, Table 3, and related significant scenarios that some of the core characteristics of a transformational leader include the following:

- **Visionary**: Obama was visionary when he said: '*... no matter what you look like, no matter where you come from, you can make it if you try*'. This statement is visionary, motivational and encouraging.

A leader must treat others with respect

- **Respectful**: A leader is expected to be accorded respect by the followers. However, it is important to acknowledge that respect must be reciprocal. It is easy for a leader to lose followers through disrespecting the latter. For example, the 2012 US Presidential Candidate Mitt Romney[33] [34] [35] appeared to have *disrespected* a 47% domain he felt would vote for Obama, no matter what, simply because they depend on the government for their welfare.

- **Team-builder**: In his first term, Obama appealed for bi-partisanship towards addressing some of the nation's challenges.

- **Inspirational**: Obama's slogan of *Yes, you can!* redefined and rekindled **hope** for the minority and the deprived.

---

[33] http://www.politifact.com/truth-o-meter/statements/2012/sep/18/mitt-romney/romney-says-47-percent-americans-pay-no-income-tax/ (Last Accessed: 06.12.2012)
[34] http://abcnews.go.com/Politics/OTUS/mitt-romneys-47-percent-pay-income-taxes/story?id=17263629#.UMESpGdCqdk
[35] http://www.politifact.com/truth-o-meter/statements/2012/sep/18/mitt-romney/romney-says-47-percent-americans-pay-no-income-tax/ (Last Accessed: 07.12.2012)

- **Trustworthy**: Obama reminded the US population, including his followers, that *I have always told you the truth*. This also relates to Honesty. A thriving community expects its 'beacon of hope' to be truthful and honest with them at all times.

- **Charismatic**: This relates to improving your image to warrant likability.

- **Honest**: A leader must start with honesty, for it forms a solid foundation on which the follower builds trust in the leader. A transformational leader must be stable and very consistent. During Mitt Romney's bid for the White House, one segment of the US population thought Mitt Romney was not being honest with them as he changed his position a number of times on important issues[36][37][38][39].

- **Empowering**: In his victory speeches, Obama empowered his followers by crediting his victory to them: *This is your victory. You did it!*

  A leader empowers others

- **Optimistic**: Being optimistic is not only about positive thinking, but also inculcating a faculty of being decisive to achieve sets of goals.

- **Reliable**: A leader must be consistent and demonstrate the ability to perform his functions under both favourable and hostile circumstances.

- **Empathetic**: Being sympathetic towards others is very human. A leader should be her/himself when showing empathy to others, for falsehood or pretence can easily be detected. It is essential for the leader to be natural.

- **Etc.**

[36] http://www.nydailynews.com/news/election-2012/mitt-romney-accused-flip-flopping-gop-backed-blunt-amendment-contraception-article-1.1031163 (Last Accessed: 10/01/2013)
[37] http://www.nydailynews.com/blogs/dailypolitics/2012/10/team-obama-plays-up-accusations-of-mitt-romney-abortion-flip-flop (Last Accessed: 10/01/2013)
[38] http://www.guardian.co.uk/commentisfree/cifamerica/2012/apr/03/mitt-romney-flip-flopper-2012 (Last Accessed: 10/01/2013)
[39]
http://www.slate.com/articles/news_and_politics/frame_game/2012/03/mitt_romney_s_contraception_flip_flop_is_a_media_created_myth_.html (Last Accessed: 10/01/2013)

5.2.3 The principles of transformational leadership

Seven principles of transformational leadership

There are seven core principles of transformational leadership that can be adapted for various functional segments (Hegar, 2012):

1. **Principle of Simplification:** This has to do with:
    i.   Where are we headed?
    ii. How do we get there?

In order to answer these questions, the transformational leader must exhibit the ability to communicate effectively and clearly on how the Vision can be achieved. The employee, team, community member or followers, must understand, without any factors that could potentially cause misunderstanding or miscommunication, that the route towards the Vision is executable. The attitude of *I misspoke*, for example, has caused many US presidential hopefuls and other leaders their candidacies. The following are two significant example lessons from vision presentation or marketing:

Example 1

A leader's vision and mission should be clear

Donald Trump, a Real Estate investor, attempted to launch a movement to question US President Obama's nationality. His attempts to expose Obama's birth certificate[40], passport and academic credentials[41] to public ridicule or scrutiny of Obama's biography fell flat[42]. Trump also initiated what others fairly saw as encouraging a revolution[43] [44] against Obama's re-election. Trump's *vision* to seek validation of Obama's birth history could be viewed to have been **communicated** rather in an

---

[40] http://www.huffingtonpost.com/2012/08/06/donald-trump-birther-obama-birth-certificate_n_1749257.html (Last Accessed: 07.12.2012)

[41] *Ibid.*

[42] http://abcnews.go.com/Politics/OTUS/donald-trump-fails-drop-bombshell-offers-cash-obama/story?id=17553670#.UMHTxKxCqSo (Last Accessed: 07.12.2012)

[43] http://abcnews.go.com/blogs/entertainment/2012/11/after-obama-victory-donald-trump-rants-on-twitter/ (Last Accessed: 07.12.2012)

[44] http://www.examiner.com/article/donald-trump-on-obama-s-re-election-total-sham-and-a-real-travesty (Last Accessed: 07.12.2012)

uncivilised and self-embarrassing[45] manner. These characteristics could draw a conclusion that although Trump is a successful business manager, he does not necessarily present the qualities of a transformational leader.

Example 2
Dr. Martin Luther King Jr, a civil rights leader, effectively communicated and marketed a well-planned vision. It took several decades, but the Promised Land **vision** Dr. King Jr effectively simplified and communicated and his *I may not get there with you… but* **we** *will get there!* have come to pass. This is because he exhibited the core (selfless) characteristics of a transformational leader, and his followers believe so much in the Vision that, they continue to emulate him.

Using **we** *in communication indicates that the leader identifies with the group*

2.   **Principle of motivation:** The leader must continuously motivate the employees, team or followers to own their work responsibilities. This will give them a sense of ownership and increase their commitment. The leader must reward the employee or team or follower's efforts and accomplishments by providing incentives or perks. In other words, a community leader must encourage the community members to own their responsibilities, rather than take a *commander* position.

3.   **Principle of determination:** The determination to succeed is not entirely up to the followers, employees or team. Much of the success is a function of how determined the leader is to achieve the envisioned goal. In Obama's 2008 quest to win the presidential race, he had to strategise in order to overcome challenging barriers such as emerging top of the Democratic Party primaries, while facing off against well-seasoned politicians (the likes of Joe Biden,

---

[45] http://www.guardian.co.uk/world/us-news-blog/2012/oct/24/donald-trump-barack-obama-records (Last Accessed: 07.12.2012)

Bill Richardson, Chris Dodd, etc., who have track records of years of experience in politics). In the face of being belittled by then presidential candidate Joe Biden, who said that the *White House is not for interns*, Obama chuckled it off and wore a broad smile. This did not only help boost his charismatic personality, but also demonstrated that he was too determined to win to allow anger mismanagement to get in the way of his Vision. In another scenario, when former Secretary of Education, Bill Richardson, lost track of a question during one of the presidential debates in the primaries, Obama spoke under low tone in repeating the question clearer to Richardson. In his determination to win, Obama courted trust from Richardson, who later chose to endorse him over Hillary Clinton.

The leader must remain determined to succeed in order to get the team to follow suit

4. Principle of mobilisation: A transformational leader must assemble a strategic team to help craft and market the Vision. The team must not be made only to believe in the Vision, but must be empowered with all the necessary tools they need to progress the agenda to reach the Vision (The Promised Land). Obama's 2008 presidential campaign teams did not only comprise 18+ year olds (US voting age), but they also mobilised much younger youth age group as low as 8 year olds. This too-young-to-vote age group believed in the Vision and helped campaign for Obama because they also believe in Obama's HOPE message that they were doing it for their future and the future of their children to come. Some of the youth on the Obama's 2008 campaign team did not even achieve the required age to vote in 2012. However, they made a huge difference as their peers or parents were likely to embrace their children's enthusiasm and have a change of heart for Obama.

Find necessary tools

5. Principle of preparation: This principle requires the transformational leader to continue learning about her/himself by her/himself as well as with the help of others, objectively. This aspect is paramount if the leader expects to be emulated by the followers or those s/he inspires.

6.   Principle of facilitation: The transformational leader must support her/his employees, team or followers with the necessary tools required to not only project the Vision, but also to lift the Vision to success. Adhering to this principle can create a win-win situation: the employees get to widen their horizon in knowledgebase; the leader's Vision is realised through an energised team.

A leader should stimulate a win-win situation

7.   Principle of innovation: The statement *Necessity is the mother of creativity (innovation)* is unarguably true. In today's agile-centric and dynamic environment, requirements (particularly human needs and demands) are constantly changing, challenging existing leadership styles to either shift in paradigm or adapt to coevolve with the uncertainties. A system's ability to cope with the changing requirements can ensure its survivability. Given the above, it is paramount for the leader to recognise the need for change and initiate the change strategically to carry the employees, team or followers along.

A leader should be innovative

5.3 Situational leadership

Unlike other leadership styles, a situational leader's approach may vary continually according to both the level of the group s/he leads and the state of the nature of the functional needs (such as working conditions or the situation), etc. This suggests that the situational leader's leadership style is greatly influenced by the needs of the group or employees s/he leads as well as the prevailing conditions of the situations in which s/he leads.

A leader must be adaptable to changes

The variability in the situational leadership style follows that the leader must be situation-oriented in terms of being flexible to adapt to any changes in the functional requirements, task, competence and commitment of the employees or group and other interconnected components, in order to achieve the goals.

5.3.1 Theoretical background

While they were researching and co-authoring the first edition of *Management of Organisational Behaviour*, Hersey and Blanchard (1969) developed the situational leadership theory. In the true sense of the meaning of the word **situation**, situational leadership suggests that there is no *universal* style of leadership that can thrive in every situation. Depending on the developmental trend of the faculty, team, group, employees or followers that the leader is leading to achieve the vision or goal, the leader must adapt her/his leadership style to the orientation of the team. In other words, it is not the group, followers or employee's responsibility to adapt to the leader's leadership style. It is rather the other way around whereby the leader should adapt to the changes in circumstances (situation) in order to drive her/his vision towards success.

5.3.2 The situational leadership model

Hersey and Blanchart (1969) developed the situational leadership model that Blanchart (1985) later refined into the well-known *The Situational Leadership II (SLII)* model. The SLII model comprises two leadership components known as the Leadership Style and the Development Level.

- **Leadership Style** (see Figure 3a), focuses on the plausible relationships that can exist between the leader and subordinate.

- **Development Level** (see Figure 3b) focuses on the competence and commitment characteristics of the subordinate.

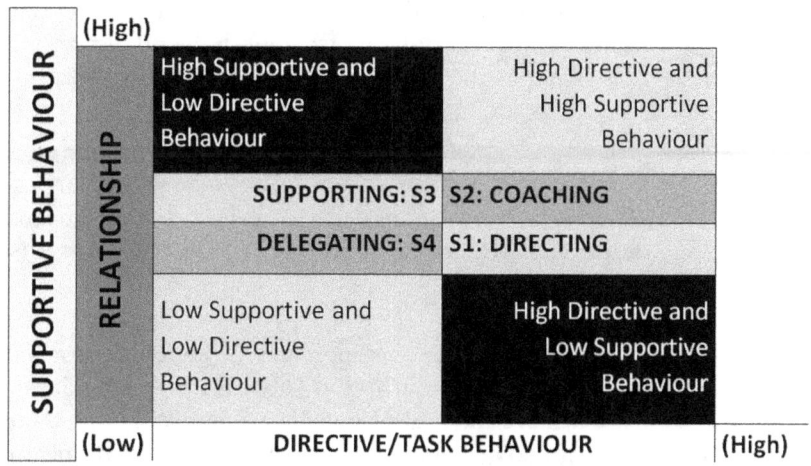

Figure 3a: The four leadership styles (Adapted from Blanchart, 1985)

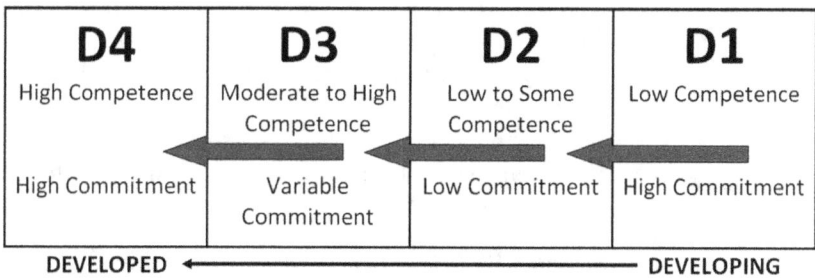

Figure 3b: Development level of the individual (Adapted from Blanchart, 1985)

Figure 3a suggests that the leadership style in this category is **behaviour-oriented** based on the relationship between the **leader** and **subordinates**; and **directive** based on the scale of the task. That is:

Supportive behaviour: As a function of the subordinate's characteristics (competence and commitment levels) with respect to the leader's relationship with the member, a two-way communication that focuses on **emotional** and **social support** exists. In this situation, the leader offers **support** to the team.

A relationship focused leader offers support to the group

Directive behaviour: Depending on the scale of the project task, the leader's focus is mainly on giving directions on the actions that must be taken by the project team members in order to accomplish the project goals. In this situation, the leader gives **directions** to the team.

The above orientations lead to classifying the situational leadership style into four groups of S1, S2, S3 and S4 (see Figure 3a):

S1. — Directing: In this approach the leader lays down the roles (actions) that the subordinate must follow to achieve the goal or complete the task. This is a **high directive behaviour** that is based mainly on accomplishing the task. In this regard, the leader provides in-depth information on the methodology required to execute the task. For such a **high** directive **one-sided** communication approach, the leader offers **low support** to the subordinate, who may be **highly committed** to the project task but has **low competence** (see D1 in Figure 3b) in the field. This domain is high task-focused. As such, the relationship between the leader and the subordinate is characterised as **low**.

S2. — Coaching: The follower in this segment shows **some level of competence** but **low in commitment** (see D2 in Figure 3b). As such, there is need for the leader to provide both coaching and support. The communication style in this domain is ideally a two-way one simply because the leader must not only provide **high directives**, but also offers **high** emotional and social **support**. Offering **high support** to the team members would influence them to buy into the leader's **directives** or method or actions to complete the project task.

S3. — Supporting: For a subordinate who demonstrates **moderate to high competence** but **variable commitment** (see D3 in Figure 3b), the leader should build a **strong relationship** with her/him. The leader and subordinate share (**participate**) in the decision-making process through a two-way communication platform. The leader appears more like a facilitator

116

since the subordinate has the capacity to carry out the task but only requires the leader's social and friendly **support** for a sustained commitment.

S4. — **Delegating**: Because the subordinate demonstrates **high competence** and **high commitment** in the project (see D4 in Figure 3b), the leader may confidently delegate the subordinate to execute the project task unsupervised. The initial communication between the leader and subordinate is primarily to discuss the project requirements and to agree on the deliverables. Therefore, the leader gives the follower the freedom to count on her/his **high** capacity and **high** commitment to accomplish the project goal.

A leader should not overburden a highly competent and committed member

5.3.3 Understanding maturity and commitment levels of the subordinate

To enable the situational leader to position her/his leadership style appropriately, s/he must be able to assess the **maturity** (i.e. competence and commitment) levels of the subordinate. Understanding the competence and commitment levels of the subordinate can help the leader identify the specific needs of the team member. This would enable the leader to not only provide the necessary support to match the follower's needs, but also to adapt her/his leadership style to the needs or **level** of the follower. The matrix in Table 4 below shows four maturity levels credited to the Hersey-Blanchard Situational Leadership Theory (Hersey, 1985).

Table 4: Hersey-Blanchard Situational Leadership Theory Maturity Levels

High	Moderate		Low
M4	M3	M2	M1
Very capable and willing	Capable but unwilling	Incapable but willing	Incapable and unwilling

The Hersey-Blanchard Situational Leadership Theory Maturity Levels (Table 4), leads to the following deductions:

M1: According to this domain, the subordinate lacks the specific skills or competence required to execute a specific project task. In addition to that, s/he has no confidence to carry out the task. The **unwillingness** or insecurity to attempt to carry out the task could significantly signal a potential exit for this follower. The follower in this category scores **Low** on the maturity scale. This suggests that if the leader delegates a task or project to someone in the M1 category, there is a likelihood that the job or project will not be done. This is a *hands-off* follower who does not present the leader with any tangible reason to be trained for the task.

It is difficult for the leader to build a sustainable relationship with an M1-person

M2: This segment does not have the prerequisite knowledge and skills background or expertise or **capacity** to undertake the task at hand. However, they are enthusiastic and **willing** to work on the task. This is a demonstration of positive attitude in that the followers in this category may be **willing** to be supported with the appropriate tools and directions to enable them develop the **capacity** they need to do the job.

An M2-person needs the leader's support to hang on

M3: This sector of followers possesses the skills (**capacity**) required to do the job at hand. However, they are not enthusiastic (**unwilling**) or confident to execute the task. Although this domain might require inspiration or motivation from the leader, they appear less passionate about the project and are likely to kill the project or cause unnecessary delays that could lead to project failure.

To keep an M3-person, the leader should be highly directive

M4: The maturity level of the individual in the M4 category is classified as **High** simply because they are not only **very competent** (**very capable**) for the project task, but they are also **willing** to execute the task. In most cases, this domain may be so enthusiastic or committed that they might require very little or no supervision to do the job. Over-burdening this group with too much work may exhaust the members in the long run. It suggests that if the leader enforces too much directives upon the follower in M4, the leader's attempt is likely to backfire. This is because the leader's action might trigger *de*motivation, leading to a loss of independence.

An M4-person is in principle in the S4 domain

Building familiarity with the Maturity Level matrix (Table 4) can help the leader to properly adjust her/his leadership skills to adapt to the needs of the project team and devise strategic approaches to stimulate the route towards success. For instance, a dysfunction may occur among workforce demographics (early 20s and mid-50s employees, for example) due to conflicting values and individual's approach to work. This can negatively affect both the team and the project success. Faced with such challenge, the leader may try to assess the **maturity** (competence and commitment) levels of individual members and the team or group as a whole (see Figure 3b). In this regard, the maturity levels of the workforce can suggest to the leader what appropriate mechanisms to explore to guide each individual follow through the project tasks.

As far as human erratic behaviours are inevitable, Table 4 might not necessarily function at all times. The following serves as an important observation worth considering:

> 'Human beings remain the most complex systems and can be very unpredictable. Although it may appear convincing that it is obviously practical to include an M4 individual in a new project, it should not come as a surprise that such **very capable** and **willing** member can at any time, without prior warning, lose interest or willingness and slip into the M3 category. This can potentially lead to project delays or failures. On the other hand, an individual initially ruled out for a new project, because of her/his M3 characteristics, might later develop an interest (**willingness**) through motivation and then cross over to the M4 category' — Melanie Flowers[46]

From the above remark it follows that the dynamic nature of humans, who can easily be influenced by external factors, suggests that there is a thin line between **willingness** and **unwillingness** that both **capable** and **incapable** individuals can cross at any time.

---

[46] Melanie Flowers, upon studying Table 4, made this observation in conversation with the author, regarding the uncertainties in human behaviourial pattern.

5.4 Contingency-based leadership

By definition, contingency theories:

hold that leadership effectiveness is related to the interplay of a leader's traits or behaviours and situational factors (Seyranian, 2012).

In essence, this definition suggests that the effectiveness of a person's leadership style is contingent upon:

- the internal situation (i.e. the interaction or relationship between the leader and project group members) and
- the external situation (the interactive factors in the environment in which the task/project is carried out)

5.4.1 Theoretical background

Originally developed by Fred Fiedler after studying various leadership types, Fiedler's Contingency Theory of Leadership (Fiedler, 1964; Fiedler *et al*, 1993) suggests that the effectiveness of leadership depends on the interaction between the following two factors: the leader's task or relations motivation and the nature of the situation.

1. The leader's task or relations motivation: Fielder noted that stress management is a key index of a leader's effectiveness. For instance, if a stressful, uncooperative, hostile or unfriendly relationship exists between the leader and group members or project team members, it will directly and negatively impact the performance output of both the group and the effectiveness of the leader.

2. Nature of the situation: According to the contingency theory, the effectiveness of the subordinates is a function of how the leader adapts her/his leadership style to the maturity (competence and commitment) level of the individual members in the project group as well as the requirements of the situation/environment (Hersey, 1985; Fiedler and Garcia, 1987; and Fiedler *et al.*, 1993).

5.4.1.1 The least preferred coworker (LPC)

In order for the leader to determine what the follower, project team or group has to do to be categorised as **primary contingency** factor, Fiedler designed the Least Preferred Coworker (LPC) model to highlight the most effective leadership style to employ contingent to a particular situation or circumstance. In effect, the model finds the correlations between the leader's orientation and her/his effectiveness.

Fiedler's LPC model (see Table 5) invites the leader to rate a past or present **co-worker** the leader has worked or works with **least** well. Individuals who score an average **high LPC** are very likely to be passion-driven and motivated to inculcate a culture of having a healthy interpersonal relationship. In essence, a leader who is relationship-focused would endeavour to establish a good relationship with the subordinates. A task-oriented leader may not necessarily focus on building any strong cordial relationship with the subordinates (i.e. **low LPC**).

The effectiveness of a leader depends on how style matches situation

Table 5: Fiedler's Least Preferred Co-worker (LPC) model

Personality Trait	Scale								Personality Trait
Unfriendly	1	2	3	4	5	6	7	8	Friendly
Uncooperative	1	2	3	4	5	6	7	8	Cooperative
Hostile	1	2	3	4	5	6	7	8	Supportive
Backbiting	1	2	3	4	5	6	7	8	Loyal
Untrustworthy	1	2	3	4	5	6	7	8	Trustworthy
Disagreeable	1	2	3	4	5	6	7	8	Agreeable
Argumentative	1	2	3	4	5	6	7	8	Compromising
...	1	2	3	4	5	6	7	8	...
...	1	2	3	4	5	6	7	8	...
Inconsiderate	1	2	3	4	5	6	7	8	Considerate
Unkind	1	2	3	4	5	6	7	8	Kind
Grumpy	1	2	3	4	5	6	7	8	Cheerful

Guarded	1 2 3 4 5 6 7 8	Open
Distant	1 2 3 4 5 6 7 8	Cold
Boring	1 2 3 4 5 6 7 8	Interesting
Egocentric	1 2 3 4 5 6 7 8	Empathic

It is worth noting, however, that in the face of cultural diversity, divergent scholarly views, norms and mores, the interpretation of the LPC scale may be subjected to controversy. Nonetheless, the LPC scale can be adapted to suit any culture-values-biased situation, etc., and explored to improve the performance of the project group as well as enable the leader to chart her/his leadership style to the ideal **situation** type. Within these confines, Fiedler deduced that, if

- the leader is accepted and accorded **respect** by the project group members or follower (that is, if a **good leader-member relationship** exists);
- the task is **well-structured** and properly delegated to the project group members; and
- a significant degree of **authority** or **power** is formally given to the leader,

then the **situation** under which the project or task is executed is deemed to be **favourable** for the leader to succeed (Fiedler, 1964; Fiedler and Garcia, 1987; Fiedler *et al.*, 1993).

5.4.2 Understanding Fiedler's LPC model

To gain an appreciable understanding of Fiedler's **LPC model** and associated **situational favourableness** deduction, it is worth considering the following three basic steps.

Step 1: Identifying your leadership style

In order to identify your leadership style, you should first assess what your primary focus is. First, do you focus on accomplishing the task? In other words, are you **task-oriented**? Secondly, do you focus on building relationships with the team members? In other words, are you **relationship-focused**? While you ponder over your responses to the above questions, do the following:

A leader may be task- or relationship-focused

   i. Answer the following question: *Who have you **least** enjoyed working with or who do you **least** enjoy working with?*

   ii. Refer to the LPC model in Table 5. Rate your experience with this person(s) in (i) on the 8-point bipolar individual personality trait scale.

   iii. Find the average in ii.

   iv. If the average is in the neighbourhood of 7 and 8 or 7.5, for example, then the LPC model suggests that you are **relationship-focused** (i.e. high LPC), otherwise you are **task-oriented** (i.e. low LPC, average score).

Are you high LPC or low LPC?

Step 2: Identifying your situation

Recall that according to the contingency theories, *the effectiveness of a leadership approach is a function of the situational factors* (Seyranian, 2012). As such, it is important to identify the **situation** in which you intend to lead. A basic approach to making this assessment is to answer the following three basic questions:

   i. Is the project task you are undertaking **structured** (organized) or **unstructured** (unorganized)? This will depend on your experience in the project field.

   ii. Is your authority or influence over the project team **strong** or **weak**?

   iii. Do you consider **leader-member** relationships **good** or **poor**?

Step 3: Determining the effective leadership style

Scenario #1: Refer to the questions in Step 2.

Let us assume that:
1. The project task is **structured**.
2. As the **leader** you are the boss, and as such your authority over the project team is **strong**.
3. Your relationship with the team is **poor**.

In a **situation** where you have **poor relationship** with the **team members**, the Fiedler LPC model suggests that you should be *relationship-focused* first. From this, it follows that for you to be very effective in this **situation** that suggest a **high LPC**, you should set off by first building a good rapport with the team you lead. As the project task is **structured** and you have a **strong** power over the team, it translates that there is a likelihood that you will ensure that the job gets done. However, in order to trigger enthusiasm in the team members so that they work with passion or earn their respect, it is important to build a **good relationship** with them at the beginning.

Scenario #2: Refer to the questions in Step 2.

Let us assume that:
1. The project task is **unstructured**.
2. As the **leader** you are the boss, and as such your authority over the project team is **strong**.
3. Your relationship with the team is **good**.

In a **situation** where you have an **unstructured** (unorganized) project task, the effectiveness of your leadership style should place emphasis on getting the job done (i.e. task-oriented). In such a **situation**, it is essential to subscribe to **low LPC**. The danger in soliciting **high LPC** is that, if you focus on building a **strong relationship** with a team engaged in an **unstructured** project task, you are likely to make compromises that might undermine the project task schedules. Your leadership style in this region must be directive in order to get the job done.

Concluding remarks:

In developing your leadership style, you may ideally adapt the various leadership characteristics and approaches (participatory, transformational, situational and contingency-based) presented in this chapter in combination with others to suitably design and plan a feasible approach to address leadership challenges within specific situations or circumstances in the domain (organisation, community, etc.) in which you wish to lead.

Study questions for Chapter 5

1. Discuss in-depth why participative leadership is considered as a sustainably democratic style of leadership.
2. Identify an important leadership problem in your organisation or community and describe how you would employ the participative leadership style to democratically address the problem.
3. In comparison to other leadership styles in Chapter 5, outline how participatory leadership style inculcates the core values of democracy.
4. Concisely define transformational leadership in your own words.
5. What are the characteristics of a transformational leader?
6. Identify a transformational leader in your organisation or community, and briefly discuss her/his leadership characteristics in the context of democratic values.
7. Identify and discuss the merits and demerits of transformational leadership within the domain of democracy.
8. Identify and, citing examples where necessary, discuss the four steps in the transformational leadership matrix. How does each step align with the fundamental principles of democracy?
9. Is transformational leadership ideal to build collaborative organisations, industries or communities? Discuss your response, featuring the important elements of democracy.
10. Are the seven principles of transformational leadership applicable to achieve harmony at your workplace, in your community or your organisation? Explain in detail, interweaving your response with the core values of democracy.
11. Situational leadership styles may be perceived as:
    i. Positive (i.e. the leader is seen as focusing on selected followers and their benefits)
    ii. Negative (i.e. the leader is seen as focusing on her/himself and for the benefit of self. In addition, the leader seems to be putting her/himself above her/his followers. In essence, s/he *controls* the followers).

    Identify and analytically discuss the factors of the positive and negative perceptions of situational leadership styles.

12. Refer to the Hersey-Blanchard Situational Leadership Theory Maturity Level matrix and explain why a leader in your organisation or department or community failed to achieve a development-oriented goal or vision. Making references to the core elements of democracy

covered in the first three chapters of this book, clearly outline what you as a leader would have done differently to achieve the goal or vision.

13. How would you, as the main Leader, deal with a key project leader who suddenly crosses over from M4 to M3 category just after completing 75% of the project work?

14. In defining situational leadership, discuss how the situational leadership style can be adapted to democratically address your organisational, institutional, or community's needs.

15. Define contingency-based leadership. How would you adapt the LPC model to democratically achieve your vision for your organisation or community's development.

16. If your organisation or community is to overcome its challenges to thrive, what type of leadership (not limited to those listed in Chapter 5) do you reckon your organisation or community would need? Discuss your answer in-depth, incorporating the fundamental principles of democracy.

17. How would you adapt each or a combination of the four leadership styles in Chapter 5, to democratically achieve your vision or goal for your school, organisation, business company or community?

18. Describe what your democratic leadership style could look like.

References

Barker, A.M, D.T Sullivan, M.J Emery (2006): *Leadership Competencies for Clinical Managers: The Renaissance of Transformational Leadership.* Sudbury, MA: Jones and Bartlett.

Burns, J Macgregor.(2003): *Transforming Leadership: A New Pursuit of Happiness.* New York: Atlantic Monthly Press.

Chemers, M.M (2002): *Cognitive, social, and emotional intelligence of transformational leadership: Efficacy and Effectiveness.* In Riggio, R.E, S.E Murphy, F. J Pirozzolo (eds.), Multiple Intelligences and Leadership.

Fiedler, F.E and J.E Garcia (1987): *New Approaches to Leadership, Cognitive Resources and Organizational Performance,* New York: John Wiley and Sons.

Fiedler, F. E, F.W Gibson and K.M Barrett (1993): *Stress, Babble, and the Utilization of the Leader's Intellectual Abilities,* Leadership Quarterly 4(2): 189–208.

Fielder, F. E (1964): 'A theory of leadership effectiveness'. In L. Berkowitz (ed.) *Advances in experimental social psychology.* New York: Academic Press.

Hegar, K.W (2012): *Modern Human Relations at Work,* 11 ed. South-Western, Ohio.

Hersey, P (1985): *The Situational Leader.* New York, NY: Warner Books.

Hersey, P and K.H Blanchard (1969): *Management of Organizational Behavior – Utilizing Human Resources.* New Jersey/Prentice Hall.

Gardiner, J.J (20069: *Transactional, Transformational, and Transcendent Leadership: Metaphors Mapping The Evolution Of The Theory And Practice Of Governance,* Kravis Leadership Institute Leadership Review, Vol. 6, 2006. pp. 62-76.

Judge, T.A., R.F Piccolo and T Kosalka (2009): *The bright and dark sides of leader traits, A review and theoretical extension of the leader trait paradigm.* The Leadership Quarterly, 20(6), 855-875.

Kouzes, J and B Posner (2007): *The Leadership Challenge.* CA: Jossey Bass.

Lewin, K, R Lippit and R.K White (1939): *Patterns of Aggressive Behavior in Experimentally Created Social Climates.* Journal of Social Psychology, 10, 271-301.

Northouse, P. G (2010): *Leadership: Theory and Practice*, 5th Edition. Sage Publications.

Pride, W.M, R.J Hughes and J.R Kapoor (2012): *Business*, 11th Edition. South-Western, Cengage learning, USA.

Ricketts, C and J.C Ricketts (2011): *Leadership: Personal Development and Career Success*, 3rd Edition. Delmar, Cengage Learning, USA.

Seyranian, V (2009): *Contingency Theories of Leadership.* Encyclopedia of Group Processes & Intergroup Relations. Eds. J.M. Levine and M.A. Hogg. Thousand Oaks, CA: SAGE, 2009. 152-56. SAGE Reference Online. Web. 30 Jan. 2012.

Chapter 6

DEVELOPING LEADERSHIP CORE COMPETENCE

There is an element of leadership ability in every individual. For instance, if you often find yourself pointing other potential leaders in the right direction, then you should acknowledge that it takes a leadership faculty to identify and catalogue the weaknesses and strengths in other leadership structures. This chapter is designed to help you identify and work on the core elements you require to develop your own leadership style.

There is an element of leadership ability in everyone

6.1 Assessing your thoughts on leadership

As a leader, your judgment or thoughts affect your mode of processing information, which will manifest in the decisions you make. For instance, if your thoughts are emphasized by fear, insecurity, pessimism and other related emotions (Mandel, 1986), then your decisions are likely to evolve from such personality traits. For instance, why would a George W. Bush leadership style go to war easily compared to an Obama leadership trait that may discourage war and seek an end to a war he did not wage? Answering the following questions may help you to partially assess your thoughts on leadership:

I.   Do you find yourself pointing a finger at the flaws in leaders?

II.   How often do you find leaders diverting from the **change** they had promised?

III.   What is your perspective of good leadership?

IV.   Do you want to take up a leadership role and later become another statistic (i.e. short-lived leadership) or look forward to a long-term leadership?

V.   What would you do to stay stainless (unscrupulous behaviour is a stain in leadership)?

6.1.1 Reassessing your thoughts about leadership

Revisit your responses to the five questions in 6.1 to check as to whether the core principles of democracy (recall chapters 1 – 3) are embedded in them. If not, enrich your responses to feature the fundamental values of democracy.

6.2. Assessing your personality

A leader should know her/his characteristics

As your personality characteristics (both inherent and developed) will influence your leadership style, it is important for you to be able to observe your personality and outline the elements that describe *you*. To enable you index your personality, do the following recommended exercises as objectively as you can.

Exercise One:

Grab a few A-4 sheets, and describe your personality in the third person. Write down all the positives and negatives about you, in the matrix format illustrated in Table 6 below.

Table 6: Your personality traits

My Personality Traits	
Positive	**Negative**
Supportive	Authoritative
Friendly	Hostile
...	...

Do not leave out how you treat others you consider lower than you, etc. Describe your personality as if you are another person writing about *you*. Be fair and objective!

Exercise Two:

Ask a few friends and/or acquaintances to write about you. You may select 2 friends and 2 acquaintances or as many as desired, and ask each of them to write about your personality. Ask them to be as fair as possible, and they should make their submissions either by hand delivery, email or post. Assure your friends and acquaintances that you need their fair judgments to help you identify the flaws in your personality, and that you do not intend to hold against them anything negative they write about you. They should have your word that their assessments would help you shape your lifestyle and perception about others. However, there is need to make room for eventualities in that respondents, given cultural diversities, might not feel comfortable to provide objective feedbacks. Some might choose not to respond at all or be bias towards you, in order not to offend. If you cannot guarantee receiving honest opinions from others about you, skip Exercise Two.

Seek the opinions of others to help you learn more about yourself

Exercise Three:

Read aloud to yourself what you wrote about yourself in Exercise One and what your friends and acquaintances wrote about your personality in Exercise Two, if any. Allow your *innerself* to listen attentively as you read.

Exercise Four:

Referring to the collective information in Exercise Three about your personality, grab a fresh sheet of paper and compile a list of all the positive things about your personality, and on another sheet write down all the negative things about you.

Exercise Five:

A leader should develop a refined personality to be a good role model

The negative things that characterise one aspect of your personality are the things you must strive to put under your control. What is not under your control is on display any time you are about. You need to put your negative elements under your control to enable you to diminish or even better to get rid of them entirely. This is a giant step to polishing your personality. You owe your friends and acquaintances gratitude for making you aware of some of the characteristics about you that you are otherwise not deeply aware of.

Exercise Six:

Send a **Thank You Note** to each of your friends and acquaintances for making you aware of some of your personality flaws. Learn to appreciate those who point you to your flaws, for they contribute to shape you as a leader.

6.3 Building communication, negotiation and public speaking skills

Are you a Public Speaker in your capacity as a leader? The answer is indeed *YES*, you are. Whether you lead a small team to manage a mini project in your community or organisation, you would often find yourself communicating your ideas to more than one person. Publicly. In this regard, if you suffer from glossophobia (fear of public speaking) this is the time to lose that fear and develop good communication skills. The people you lead are in the public and so your speeches are public. As a leader, you will be expected to possess the ability to communicate your vision effectively. In this regard, you may need to improve your public speaking ability.

How do you build public speaking skills? A good leader must be a good listener. Not only must you communicate effectively, but you must also learn to listen effectively and process information within the shortest reasonable time. Start off by first learning how to listen actively, and then learn how to communicate effectively. Active listening and effective communication skills are key ingredients for well-connected public speaking.

A good leader is a good listener

6.3.1 Developing active listening and communication skills

Active listening is very important for **effective communication**. It demonstrates that you (leader) are actively (not passively) listening to others (subordinates or followers or group) attentively and with interest by:

- Giving feedbacks, using keywords that resonate with your audience,
- Making eye contact,
- Nodding (courteously and genuinely) where necessary,
- Etc.

Active listening focuses more on the audience, follower, group or subordinate than on the leader (boss, etc.). Imagine a scenario where you overheard one of your subordinates telling another colleague: *'My doctor listens, my attorney listens, my mentor listens, my carpenter listens, my chimney sweeper listens, but my boss does not listen.'* — Unknown

Or imagine a time when you heard your son tell his uncle, in your presence: *'My mum does not listen to me.*

In order to develop listening and communication skills, the following suggestions are worth considering:

1. **Be natural.** Be yourself to allow people to connect with you rather than getting them to compare you with the one you are imitating.

2. **Listen to ideas.** Do not memorise facts. By making an effort to listen to the ideas others present and making constructive reference to them, you get to make them (subordinates) feel important too. This will earn you a good relationship with those you lead.

3. **Don't lead with one head.** As a leader, you must avoid the mistake of having only one thinking head on your shoulders. Do not get people to think that, in your sole opinion, you are the only one with a brain. Avoid silencing others by showing off or boasting with your qualifications and authority over the subject, as if you own the turf and all others should keep off. This is a negative attitude that will quickly portray you as an arrogant, *non-listening authoritative leader.* A smart leader is the leader who makes use of all the heads of those s/he leads. Treat the people you lead with respect, flexibility, dignity and equality and you would be amazed to learn how much you could learn from their great ideas to help drive your leadership in the right direction.

A good leader treats others with a sense of equality

4. **Build rapport.** Rapport is about connecting with your audience. You need to build rapport with your audience, for that leads to a good/strong bond between you and the potential follower. One way of achieving this is for you to

improve on how you listen and understand people, and then work on flexibility. If you fail to build good rapport, then your speech or presentation is potentially a waste of everybody's time and resources. For example, if your audience (a prospective follower, for example) thinks her meeting with you the previous week was **excellent**, then do not use a *mismatch* keyword in your response such as *Oh yeah, that was* **cool**. The keyword **excellent** is higher in importance than the word **cool**. Your response suggests to your audience that you probably did not value your previous meeting as she did. This puts off the prospective follower, and could suggest an early exit for her. Thus, a response such as *Oh yeah, that was very* **great** is likely to not only resonate with the prospective follower, but also put a smile across her face.

5.   **Be clear.** Be clear in what you want to achieve (goal or vision), for the clearer you are the better. An effective way is to know your audience, for that would help you to resonate well with the audience by selecting the appropriate words to convey your message. For example,

i. If your audience is a visual person or visionary, you might want to paint words with graphic details and use words or phrases like the following:

- Do you see what I mean?
- Picture this
- Imagine this
- Let me highlight
- Etc.

ii. If the audience is auditory, then the following sound words would appeal to auditory persons:

- Does this sound good to you?
- How does this resonate?
- Does this strike a chord?
- Etc.

iii. If the audience is kinaesthetic, then the following feel-oriented words may suffice:

- Do you have a feel for this?
- Does it grab you?

- Get a handle on this
- Etc.

*A leader
should
recognize the
audience's
preference*

Recognising your **audiences' preference** is important, for it will enable you to communicate effectively by connecting with each of them. This will demonstrate your ability to respect the people you lead by using the appropriate keywords that help them understand your message. In this way you would be able to not only build a good rapport, but also convey your message without drowning the audience in a sea of jargons they do not understand. How do you know your audience's preference? The best approach is to listen to them attentively in order to identify their preferences through the words (keywords) they use. Another innovative way is to get them to tell you a short story to enable you tap into their preferences. You will observe that visual persons would usually roll or direct their eyes up to the ceiling or to a corner in order to picture the information they are processing. They do so to avoid being distracted by the many actions around them. This is something you must understand and respect to prevent yourself from misjudging an audience who is staring at the ceiling while you are talking. If you force such a person to look you in the eyes while you talk, then you would get them distracted and they would not be able to process the information you are giving them. You will break the opportunity to connect with such an audience, if you force them to listen your way. Auditory thinkers will usually look straight ahead when they are pondering. Kinaesthetic will tend to look down when they are thinking for that helps them to get in touch with their feelings.

*A good
leader gives
and seeks
feedback*

6. **Give feedback and solicit feedback.** It is important to give feedback to those you listen to by using the words (keywords) that are very important to them. You should also solicit feedback to ensure you help them understand your message clearly and fully.

7. **Ask effective questions.** There are two types of questions that define the effectiveness or friendliness of your questions. They are Closed Questions (CQ) and Open

Questions (OQ). The following are typical examples to illustrate CQs and OQs:

- Is that all you want to talk about? – CQ
- What else is there to talk about? – OQ

- Did you enjoy this? – CQ
- What did you enjoy about this? – OQ

- Can you solve that? – CQ
- How can you get this done? – OQ

- Will it be done by Monday? – CQ
- When will it be done? – OQ

Recommended:

To enable your audience to loosen up and speak freely, use **open questions** (OQ) for they are more friendly than **closed questions** (CQ).

A good leader uses OQs

6.3.2 Public speaking dos and don'ts

Effective listening and communication skills can create and cement a good relationship between you (the leader) and your followers (subordinates). As such, you must avoid pitfalls (such as public relation disasters) that could compromise the relationship. In order to avoid PR mines, it is important to widen your horizon of the **Dos** and **Don'ts** of public speaking

A leader should avoid PR disasters mines

Do not focus on *you*, but *them* (followers).

It is not about you, but those you lead. As a (public) leader, you are not leading 'you' but others in your organisation or community. It is not about you so do not start your public speech by presenting a catalogue of your personal achievements (such as, the number of academic degrees you have attained, how extensively you've travelled the world, how much cash you put into constructing your dream house, etc.). Talk about how your leadership ideas would benefit the organisation or your community or those (subordinates, followers) listening to you. For example, it is better to prevent yourself from saying:

I invested £500,000 in research to develop Service X...

to rather use a less boasting statement such as:

We have developed Service X to help you design your own custom service for your community development.

Tell a true story and make a point.

Your leadership style and decisions will affect the future of the people you lead in your organisation or community. As such, you cannot afford to use a fictional story to make a point you expect to work for people in the real world. If you want to be taken seriously but do not have a true personal story to tell, then research real life scenarios in stories you wish to use to illustrate a point that could potentially address a challenge in your organisation or community.

Do not speak loosely, if your speech is unscripted.

Be a thoughtful speaker

If your presentation or speech is unscripted, then be thoughtful before you speak. Often when leaders speak loosely, they make bad news headlines and they find themselves making the following ridiculous excuses:

- I misspoke
- I was misquoted
- I was caught in the moment
- My words were twisted to mean otherwise
- I was exhausted after giving 1001 interviews
- I am happy to say sorry if my statement hurts anyone

- I can explain
- That was not what I meant
- Everyone makes mistakes
- Etc.

Do not lose your audience.

Know your audience and respect their levels of education. This would enable you to demonstrate courtesy, equality and diplomacy. Based on their level, adopt the appropriate language and tone to help them understand you. If, for example, the vast majority of the people in your community have not gone past secondary school education, then avoid using difficult-to-understand terms or words. It is not a strategic and smart way to impress your community by using advanced technical terms that could silence or confuse them. The last thing you would want to do is leave your audience at sea at the end of your speech.

Respect your audience

Do not overload your audience with too much information.

Avoid overloading your audience with loads of information at very short or no intervals. Keep the information simple and allow a brief space of time to enable them to process the information before you move on to the next point. If you talk and talk and talk and talk without allowing them time to think in-between, you would bore them to death and they would be happy to either clap you off the stage or pray for the nightmare to be over.

Allow your audience time to process your message

Connect with your audience.

Do not bond only with your power point presentation or scripted speech paper or the conference room. Remember that the audience is your target and so you need to connect more with them. Let your audience understand that your presentation is for them and that you wish for *you* and *them* to be on the same wavelength.

You can build an excellent rapport with your audience by getting them involved from the early stages. Do not be too conventional by waiting for the *Are there any questions?* moment at the end of your presentation. Do not delay their participation. I recalled attending an interesting online (Skype) business presentation. A number of ideas and questions came to mind. I eagerly waited for *Are there any questions or comments?* at the end of the presentation. My hope to participate was dashed when the presenter said, at the end of her information-loaded presentation, that:

If anyone has a question, he or she should email me or go to my blog to post their question.

Give your audience a chance to participate actively

Make your presentation as participatory as possible, for that is characteristic of participative leadership and democracy.

6.4 Widening your horizon

6.4.1 Short to mid-term leadership

If you allow your core strengths (personal traits and acquired skills) to be limited by your current level of knowledge (horizon), then you would have difficulty coping with the rapid dynamics of change in your community. If you do not go past your current horizon, your leadership style would be relegated to a short-term type. Educate yourself to keep up with the changing trends of the environment. If, for instance, you're used to attending conferences in person and now there is demand to cut costs, then be prepared to learn the basic technology that would enable you to attend conferences online. Web conferencing, for instance, is the technology in this sense. Educating yourself to build new skills to add to what you already have, will help you move from short-term to mid-term.

6.4.2 Going past your mid-term leadership

On landing on the mid-term pad, do not get complacent. Time flies along with change and your additional knowledge and skills will be tested as time goes by. To excel in the mid-term phase and be in control of your leadership skills, you must endeavour to continuously improve your skills and widen your knowledge. This means you must work both within and outside your domain. Stepping out of your comfort zone could challenge you to learn new things. For example, if you work as a school teacher in your community, you may also want to work as a volunteer support staff at your local Disability Centre. The latter will give you the opportunity to access a new knowledge in disability care, disability rights laws, equality, human dignity, and human rights, etc. Such a revelation, for example, will help you to expand your leadership manifesto to include increased services for the physically challenged.

6.4.3 Mid-term to long-term leadership

For a long-term leadership role, you must seek continuing professional development or career enhancement learning schemes. Never stop learning. Educating yourself or allowing your brain to learn new things does not only sharpen your intellectual faculty, but also increases your chances of lasting longer as a leader. If employees will normally count on you for guidance to enable them meet all requirements for enhanced performance in the workplace, for instance, then as a leader you must

Be willing to seek further education in areas where you are weak

demonstrate what you tell others to do. If this falls within your leadership environment, then do well to acquire an in-depth knowledge or study in Human Resource Management. This will give you the tools you need to help others balance work with their personal lives. If your leadership requires you to lead projects in your organisation or community, whether mini or major, then you must be conversant with project management skills in order to be literally involved (not merely directing work traffic to others). Would a study in Sustainability Management help your long-term leadership plan? If yes, then plan for further studies in Sustainability Management.

Are you the motivational powerhouse many turn to for coaching or mentorship? Whether you are born with it or not, seek the appropriate training to help you excel in coaching and mentorship. Taking up a coaching course, if that is your field, would help you identify tested tools your mentees need to translate their challenges into opportunities. As a motivational powerhouse or leader, you are also a keynote or public speaker. Even if you are born a natural speaker, it will benefit you to get proper coaching from the professionals in public speaking.

Re-examine your knowledge and core strengths with respect to the community or environment in which you want to lead. If you need to increase your knowledge and skills in areas where you are weak, then do not hesitate to increase your knowledge and skills through continuing professional enhancement or development training schemes. Find the topic or subject you need to master in order to function adequately. This attitude is a recipe for preparing for long-term leadership.

6.4.4 Helping others thrive

As you strive to widen your horizon to cement your chances of achieving excellence in your leadership ability, remember to help the people you lead to do the same. Encourage others to also expand their knowledgebase and skills. Through mentorship, *you* as a leader can support your community members to acquire additional resources through capacity-building, etc.

Empower your followers

As a good leader, you do not want to be seen as the only one who has the ability to learn. In particular, a democratic leader does not want to be stuck with people who are not prepared to step out of their comfort zones for the betterment of their lives. You would expect those you lead to also thrive, don't you? To help your mentees or followers or subordinates tap into the leadership potential within them, pay key attention to the keywords they mention when it comes to discussing certain subjects. Pay attention to what is important to them. That is, the issues they talk about with passion. Such key issues may include:

Pay attention to the issues that matter to the team members

- Areas where they excel or want to excel.
- Special skills or talents they may possess.
- Inner resources they have not explored.

As you listen attentively to your mentees or those you lead, make a list of their keywords (traits and/or learned behaviours or characteristics/or wishes) and design means to help them unleash their untapped potential or achieve excellence. Support them with the appropriate motivation and guidance that will help them subscribe to the need to widen their horizon, thrive and take up leadership roles in their fields of interest. This is tantamount to encouraging them to broaden their knowledgebase as well as take ownership of their responsibilities.

As a democratic leader, you are in no way competing with those you are leading. Your core task is to help them achieve growth, independence, and confidence to also lead others. You can start by individually asking your followers or subordinates the following questions:

1. What are your core strengths and weaknesses?
2. Do you have any known talents that you have not fully explored?
3. What are the things you want to do with your potential or talents or knowledge?
4. What is hindering (threatening) you from exploring your talents or skills?
5. What do you know/have that you think others would want to have/know about?
6. What are your challenges/limitations?

Help others add value to their lives

By helping others harness their inner resources constructively, you will accomplish a great deal by helping (leading) others to add value to their lives. Their success is your and the community's reward. Your success will manifest in a 'Team Community'.

Study question for Chapter 6

How important are effective communication, negotiation skills, public speaking ability and active listening to democratic leadership?

Reference

Mandel, R (1986): *Psychological Approaches to International Relations, Political Psychology.* Ed. Margaret Hermann, San Francisco: Jossey-Bass.

PART THREE

DEMOCRACY AND LEADERSHIP COMBINED

Chapter 7

LINKING DEMOCRACY AND LEADERSHIP

Linking leadership and democracy for the betterment of your community and those you lead or plan to lead, is a matter of marrying your leadership style with the fundamental values of democracy (recall Chapters 1 – 3). Understanding and mastering the fundamental principles of democracy can help both shape and position you for a democratic leadership role. The following recommended action plans may be helpful in shaping your leadership platform – and your daily life as a citizen and a human being.

7.1 Suggested actions to take

7.1.1 Action #1: Imbibe the values of democracy

1.   **Keep your faculty alert of democracy.** In keeping your faculty sharpened with the meaning of democracy, you are positioned to promote equality for all. The UN's Universal Declaration of Human Rights is a good source of information that would widen your understanding of human rights and needs, and how these may contribute to a better society and better life for yourself and the people around you.

2.   **Accord others with respect.** Just as you expect your followers to recognize your position and give you the full

respect you deserve, you must also acknowledge the need to recognize human dignity and give others the full respect they deserve.

3. Familiarize yourself with the dimensions and foundations of democracy. Described in-depth in Chapter 1, the dimensions and foundations of democracy can help you feature essential elements in your democratic leadership style. For example, it will help you to appreciate the need to seek democratic decision-making as suggested in participatory leadership theory. This approach promotes equal rights and equal opportunities for all.

4. Stimulate two-way communication. A two-way communication in life and leadership can be achieved through a sense of **reciprocity**, described in Chapter 2. **Reciprocity** allows others the opportunity to speak and be listened to. It demonstrates **respect** for others. People often feel disrespected when they are given reason to believe that they are not worth listening to.

Let others feel they are worth listening to

5. Promote reconciliation. To achieve a state of perfection where we remain infallible is difficult – or even unattainable. As human beings we are susceptible to err. We hurt ourselves and hurt others through our errors. However, in order for us to thrive in harmony, there is the need to acknowledge our shortcomings and render apologies. It is humbling for a leader to acknowledge her/his faults and seek forgiveness from those s/he victimizes. But it must be done, and its benefits grow with practice.

Apologies have benefits that grow

6. Do not deprive others of material goods. As presented in Chapter 2, humans also depend on material goods for their welfare. It is therefore a responsibility of a community leader to ensure that s/he protects the resources the community members count on for their survival.

7. Observe human rights. As a citizen and democratic leader, it is your core responsibility to recognize that every human being has a fundamental right to have access to food, good health, education, freedom from any form of discrimination, etc.

Do not deny others of their rights

8. **Promote human development.** As you better your competence to lead others, you should also endeavour to help others develop beyond their current states. This creates a balance and harmony in the community.

9. **Be supportive of human security.** As a democratic leader, your subordinates look up to you to ensure their security. The *self-first* stance all the war leaders took during the 14 year civil war in Liberia weakened both internal and border security structures, exposing the innocent to countless kill fields.

10. **Do not limit democracy to a 'Western only' concept.** As demonstrated in Chapter 3, democracy is universal and has been in existence and practice before the West became known as such. The principles of democracy are built on the concept of human dignity and are logical consequences thereof.

Democracy knows no bounds

7.1.2 Action #2: Avoid character mines

1. **Map out your negative characteristics.** Consciously fine-tune and preserve your good personality. Expand your positive characteristics and lose your negative elements.
2. **Brand your name and personality** through becoming a consistent leader. Exhibiting an on-and-off personality could turn you into an unstable leader. Allow your good natured personality to be consistent in everything you do so that your name can become synonymous with a *good and consistent personality.*
3. **Avoid destructive character mines.** Your good personality will be tested in so many ways. In order to avoid stepping on any mines, you must remain principled for the benefit of your community and the international society. Demonstrate the personality you would want to see in democratic leaders. Examples of destructive character mines you must avoid include:

Avoid character mines

- Disrespecting fellow human beings
- Depriving others of human dignity

- Abusing human rights
- Being corrupted
- Corrupting others
- Inculcating a culture of bribery
- Adopting immoral lifestyle
- Creating premises for scandals
- Falling for any scandals
- Going back to any of your past negative attitudes
- Being undemocratic
- Being dictatorial

7.1.3 Action #3: Keep an **open mind**[47]

1. A **closed mind**, the opposite of **open-mindedness**, is an almost impenetrable iron curtain that separates you from the beauty of life, innovative ideas, appreciating others, new opportunities, reinventing yourself, etc. A closed mind will turn you into an authoritative leader because it will expand your egocentricity to the extent that no one around you are worth listening to. With a closed mind, you are always in the right. This means you will be diagnosed as suffering from the Right Syndrome. While a closed mind will get you to block others from excelling, it will also turn you into a monster. Selfishness will be characteristic of your personality, if you do not let loose of your closed-mindedness.

Avoid closed-mindedness

2. Keep an **open mind** to possibilities. Open-mindedness can help you evolve into a likeable person and a good, democratic leader. This is simply because an attitude of open-mindedness allows you to:

- Listen to others
- Support others to take initiatives
- Create opportunities for others
- Help others excel
- Let others lead

---

[47] Flowers (2012)

- Rekindle hope to your country
- Help your community develop
- Appreciate what the international society offers you and others
- Strengthen human dignity as you respect human rights, human development and human security

7.1.4 Action #4: Declare yourself a leader

1. **Declare to yourself that you are taking a leadership role:** Shoulder part of today's responsibilities by taking up a leadership role. Whether you are a refugee, teacher or graduate, your community (refugee environment, university, etc.), the country of asylum, country of resettlement, your country or the international society, is counting on you to help make a positive difference in the world. For example, the leadership structures that gave birth to the social services that benefit your family are not dependent solely on the civil servant. You are a part of the government and have a role to play. How? Your behavioural patterns can affect the decisions that drive the social services. How? If you continue to take seriously the opportunities the social services programme provide and strive to achieve excellence for the benefit of your community, you add meaning and purpose to the continued existence of the programme. Because of you and your input, your government may see the need not only to improve the social services, but also to sustain them. In this respect, your good citizenship, exemplary lifestyle and taking ownership of your responsibilities in society could help those who abuse the system to rethink their actions. Thus, declaring yourself a leader will enable you to commit yourself to an aspect of responsibility you are prepared to drive forward. Examine your core strengths and pick one area that is in need of your strengths. For example, take a close look at your community to identify the many talented young men and women who are ready, may be even waiting for your guidance. You can begin by planning a regular meeting at which time you offer free training or

Take up a leadership role

teaching in an area that would help them tap into their talents and expand their horizon.

2. **Tell others about your leadership plans.** You know yourself and have declared your intentions to *yourself.* The next thing is to *sell* your idea to others. Do not keep your leadership commitment to yourself. After all you want to help others and your community to benefit from your good intentions. Therefore, your declaration should not remain a top secret. Declare your leadership intentions and commitments to your friends. Keep an open mind. Your listeners may point you to constructive leadership responsibilities waiting to benefit from your strengths.

Let your vision for the community be a shared idea

3. **Leadership is not limited to waiting-to-occupy-a-top-position.** Leadership, married to democratic values, is generally a way of life. Understand that leadership is a shared responsibility (participative). If you find yourself pointing a finger at a leader who abuses human dignity in your community, organisation or school, make sure that you quickly do a reality check of your personality as to whether you respect human dignity and human rights in regards to the everyday people with whom you interact. As an individual, you must always inculcate the characteristics of a democratic leader because you are part of the shared responsibilities of the leadership in your organisation, school or society.

Democracy and leader-ship are a way of life

7.1.5 Action #5: Do onto others as you would want them do onto you

1. **Be ethical in all your dealings.** The question of ethical behaviour is central to democracy and leadership. How well do your keywords (leadership behaviour, characteristics, democratic values, etc.) position you to address inevitable ethical issues in your community? It is certain that your leadership characteristics will influence your integrity and provide ethical ballast for how you behave in your life and interact with your community and elsewhere. For instance, Company X in a democratic country such as the United Kingdom produces Product P in Bangladesh for sales distribution in rich and developed

countries ABC. The manufacturing source in Bangladesh employs the underaged to do the work for low pay. The leadership at Company X does not care who does what in Bangladesh as long as Product P is made at a low wage rate and delivered at low cost. Although global manufacturing may be legally and academically defined as the transfer of manufacturing resources to low wage rate countries (Flowers and Cheng 2009a, 2009b, 2011), is it ethical for the leadership at Company X to encourage child labour for the production of Product P? Besides the ethical responsibilities expected of the leadership in corporate organizations and states, it is fair to question the roles played by parents who compromise the child's rights to security (protection), education, etc. Leadership is a shared responsibility and so the parent has a role to play in this kind of child exploitation. However, the parents also see that the children's work help to put food on the family's table. Often it is the parent's decision either to accept the request for their ward to work under the age or stay in school. It may therefore be a question whether the parents who encourage their ward to be engaged in child labour should be held accountable for contributing to the abuse of the child's rights to security, education etc.

Ethical behaviour is central to democratic leadership

2. **Help dismantle any modern day slavery structures of any kind.** The United States of America prides itself of being a democratic nation since its founding days. Yet, slavery was once a legal enterprise in the US (Horter and Horton, 2004). Some leaders within democratic structures stand to benefit from modern day slavery and child labour. They seem to see their leadership as acceptable so far as *they can afford to do onto others what they will not want to be done onto them and their children.* Many so-called global businesses are *legally* benefitting from child labour (i.e. modern day slavery). None the less, all things that are legal are not necessarily ethical.

Something legal is not always ethical

Inculcating a sense of the Golden Rule, **doing onto others as you (also as a leader) would want others to do onto you** can stimulate a deep sense of ethics and daily habits that enforce human dignity. As this becomes our way of life as a person, a parent, a citizen, a leader, our lives will become increasingly rewarding to the people around us – and to ourselves.

Study questions for Chapter 7

1. Describe how you would link the principles of democracy to your leadership style.
2. Outline in detail how you would use your leadership style to democratically address a potential problem in your organisation or community.
3. Given the ongoing practice of modern-day slavery under the guise of exporting manufacturing resources to low wage rate countries, should ethical behaviour be redefined to get both international corporate leaders (such as the CEO) and domestic leaders (such as parents) to take active responsibility in protecting the rights of children?
4. Define and describe *in-depth* your leadership style.

References

Flowers, M and K Cheng (2009a): 'Global manufacturing: reconfiguration of machines in addressing changing customer requirement scenarios'. In *Journal of Applied Mechanics and Materials*, Vol. 16-19, pp. 15-19.

Flowers, M and K Cheng (2009b): *Global manufacturing: reconfiguration of machines in addressing changing customer requirement scenarios.* 7th International Conference on e-Engineering and Digital Technology, 3-5 September, Shenyang, PR China.

Flowers, M and K Cheng (2011): 'Reconfiguration as a responsive tool for the agile-centric global manufacturing domain'. In *International Journal of Internet Manufacturing and Services*, Vol. 3, No. 1, pp. 1-15.

Flowers, M (2012): *The Moneymaking Code* 5th edition. Flowers Publications.

Horter, J.O and L.E Horton (2004): *Slavery and the Making of America.* New York: Oxford University Press.

NOTES

www.ingramcontent.com/pod-product-compliance
Lightning Source LLC
Chambersburg PA
CBHW070654290526
45790CB00001B/312